Gestalt Group Therapy:

A Practical Guide

Gestalt Group Therapy:
A Practical Guide

Bud Feder

Developed and Published by Create Space Publishing and
 Ravenwood Press a subsidiary of the
Illawarra Gestalt Centre.
P.O. Box 141, Peregian Beach,
 Queensland, 4573
AUSTRALIA.

Cover illustration, text design and art work: B O'Neill

For more information on Ravenwood Press
Email: boneill@uow.edu.au
Website: www.illawarragestalt.org
Or write to

Brian O'Neill
Illawarra Gestalt
P.O. Box 141, Peregian Beach, Queensland, 4573

Table of Contents

Dedication

This little book is lovingly dedicated to Ruth Ronall, my long term partner in crime, my inspiration, my colleague, my tormentor and my friend.

Although regretfully Ruth is no longer able to participate directly in this project, there is nothing I do concerning groups in which she does not have a strong voice - unbeknownst to most, yet loud and clear to me.

x

Acknowledgements

My sincere thanks to the following who contributed to this effort either directly or indirectly:

My beloved buddies Linda DiTullio, Jack Aylward and John Flynn [deceased] with whom I ran many a rewarding and informative marathon

Stefan Hahn and Justa Bernstaedt whose perceptive questions assisted me in determining what to include in this guide

My sweet godson Corey Flynn who generously and graciously let me use his computer when mine was down

Anne Teachworth for her precise and excellent editing

The many clients who joined me in our struggles, adventures, successes and failures as group members/leaders/persons

My mentors Laura Perls, early on, and Dan Bloom, more recently

Ruth Ronall most especially and to whom this book is dedicated

Foreword

Peter Cole

A Humanist's Guide to Gestalt Group Leadership

Bud Feder has been a leader in gestalt therapy's movement toward the practice of a more process oriented, interactive approach to gestalt therapy in groups. Through his writing and teaching, he has charted a path for those of us who have sought new directions in the practice of gestalt group therapy (GGT). Having brought together the world's leading thinkers in the field of GGT in two editions of his seminal co-edited volume: Beyond the Hotseat, having written numerous articles and book chapters on GGT, having led countless workshops on GGT throughout the world, and having trained many of its leading practitioners, he brings forth a more personal side of his lifelong love affair with GGT in this honest, unpretentious and wise book.

This is a side of Bud Feder I know well, as I have had the privilege of co-leading many groups with Bud over years of collaboration with him as fellow faculty of the Sierra Institute for Contemporary Gestalt Therapy. This book is written in Bud's distinct and authentic voice: that of an unassuming yet deeply learned and committed practitioner of GGT. This book is infused with a humanity that is Bud's signature strength: the ability to bring out the best in others through a profound appreciation of all that we share.

GGT is a deeply human endeavor. Its practice touches every corner of the human condition. Bud Feder traverses this territory with a light touch and a gentle humor. But make no mistake, the territory he maps can be as treacherous as it can be rewarding, and the advice he shares is hard won from a lifetime of entering into the mysteries, surprises and challenges of the practice of GGT.

Bud brings a unique perspective to his work with groups – one that integrates a strngly democratic sensibility with an appreciation for the judicious exercise of the leader's authority. This integration helps bring the best of the gestalt therapy tradition into the realm of interactive, process-oriented group work, for it promotes dialogical relationships among all group participants: members and leaders.

I find it wonderfully fitting that Bud discusses "Team of Rivals" here: Doris Kearns Goodwin's analysis of

Abraham Lincoln's leadership of his cabinet and country during the Civil War. What Lincoln exemplified on the macro stage of politics and history, we can apply on the micro stage of gestalt group therapy: an arena that calls upon its leaders to navigate the often stormy waters of conflict, to provide leadership for strong personalities whose talents and strengths we must harness for the group's ultimate success, and to bring a sense of greater purpose to the group experience. Bud's discussion of Lincoln reminds us that some qualities of leadership transcend current theories and trends. Leadership attributes such as employing a democratic style, involving the whole group, "giving as much support as necessary and as little as possible", and judicious responsibility are timeless virtues of leadership that can serve as beacons for GGT leaders in guiding their groups.

Gestalt group therapy leaders engage in the most challenging, complex, and potentially rewarding work a therapist can undertake. Bud Feder has generously shared the core of his approach to group leadership here, and GGT leaders at all levels of experience will benefit from his vision, his hard won wisdom, and his guidance.

Peter Cole
Berkeley, CA

Preface to the Second Printing

*"I have heard talk of the beginning and the
end, but I do not talk of the beginning or the
end. There has never been more inception than
there is now"*

Walt Whitman

<u>A personal note:</u> my first effort at group leadership,
at age eleven, got mixed reviews. This was in 1941,
so it was timely that one member of our club ['*The
Philly Humbugs*'] labeled me "a Hitler" when I kicked
him out. The other guys though appreciated my
organizational energy. I didn't realize it at the time,
yet I had been bitten by the 'group bug'...and was
permanently infected.

Later the effect was more noticeable when it came to choosing a topic for my doctoral dissertation. I settled on a study of group therapy with delinquent adolescent boys. I've been involved in groups ever since – therapy groups, research groups, social clubs, as well as community and professional organizations. I even brought my interest in groups into my tennis club where I befuddled my club mates with my efforts, and finally I mention here a meditation on Lincoln and his Cabinet [see epilogue]. All background for what follows.

~~~~~~~~~~~~~~

I wrote this little book in 2006 after many years of practicing and thinking about gestalt group therapy. And I subtitled it "A Practical Guide" since that was mainly what I set out to do...to give other gestalt group therapists, particularly beginners, the benefit of the actual ways I work and the tweaks and aids I had come up with and accumulated over the years.

In the writing, it grew a bit, as in often the case for me in writing...and I suspect this is true for many writers...and for composers in composing....and for actors in acting...and for tennis players in playing, etc.

This growth in the book (or more accurately and modestly, booklet) led to the chapters (or *chapterlets*) - I always write succinctly, in fact my doctoral dissertation at Columbia University was the second shortest in the history of the university, at least at the time: 46 pages. Compare Rollo May who was in the same program as I and his 350-page doctoral thesis masterpiece *The Meaning of Anxiety*]...As I was saying this led to the early *chapterlets* on the history of, the nature of, and the justification for gestalt group therapy. It also led to my tuning up and presenting the model I had developed which guides my work [Ch. 5].

After that I focus on the nuts-and-bolts of this work... which is good insofar as and to the degree that therapy is a nuts-and-bolts endeavor. And I am glad to offer the forms and handouts I've created over the years found in Appendix A for your use and freeform adaptation as you see fit.

Of course therapy is also an art form and a person-to-person, or as my esteemed publisher might well say, a soul-to-soul encounter, sometimes dramatic and often subtle which might be better characterized as stone upon stone, slowly leading to a hopefully beautiful edifice. This is equally true in group therapy as it is in individual therapy, and otherwise why would we bother to be psychotherapists rather than dentists [no offense Paul...my dentist].

If my particular artistry comes through, that's nice. I don't know if it can through using the squiggles on paper which we call words, but if so, that's a bonus. What I do require of myself though in this *opuslet* is that some useful pointers and direction are supplied and that is what I aimed to do. If I succeeded then it's up to each therapist/artist to use the tubes of paint provided to create her/his art form.

It's a wonderful challenge and very worth the effort. It is a rare day, after 50 years of practice, that I don't enter a group session without heightened anticipation [and sometimes a lot of tension] and that I don't leave it without feeling enriched. I hope you find this useful on <u>your</u> journey.

Bud Feder

Jan. 4, 2013

Chapter 1 – A Sample Session

This 'sample' session is really a composite session, compressing together a few consecutive sessions. The idea is that I will refer back to it in subsequent chapters to illustrate what I am discussing. This is a 90-minute session in a private practice group, consisting of four men and four women, so of course not representative of all the many varieties of groups – marathons, men's groups, etc. [The comments in italics in brackets are my editorial gems].

Some background

Walt had missed the last session without any notice before or after [a violation of our agreement- a group rule]. Fortuitously I met him at the local health food market and he told me he was leaving the group. We made a deal: he would come in to say goodbye and I would do all I could to insure that nobody badgered him.

The Session starts

He did come and as it happened sat right next to Donna, who had told me in individual session that she was afraid to come back because she had been too "overwhelming and scary' to the other members – and nevertheless came even though her father that very day had been admitted to the emergency room for heart trouble. She chose the group over him.

Walt began and told the group it was his last session, explaining that he had never felt a good fit and that he didn't put much stock in feelings. I requested the group to give any personal feedback they wanted yet not to press Walt into staying. Most of the feedback was positive and after, on his own initiative, Walt did a round telling how he felt about each person [predictably bland]. I said "And what about me?" After a pause he said "I don't trust you". I suggested we explore that, yet he refused...and left for good.

A 'new' group

Recognizing that there was now a new group configuration [or system] I asked how this felt to each person. Naturally there were varied reactions. Camilla said she liked now that there were an equal number of men and women [*she was including me in the count]*. Kim expressed shakiness since the group no longer felt stable and secure – anyone could disappear at any time [*an existential reality.]* I asked her breathe into this and experiment with accepting it. Jason described the new group as feeling thinner and poorer, as for him Walt was a rich and charismatic member and he looked forward to seeing him weekly. I challenged him to put more of his own richness into the group. After all of the members had expressed themselves on Walt's leaving, I added that I was sorry he left, that I liked him and that his last comment to me about mistrusting me was disturbing and I wished we had engaged on it. I sighed.

We move on

After some silence Donna spoke up about being scared to come, as stated above. She spoke mostly in the past tense, referring to the last session in which she unloaded a lot of her troubled history: "I was testing you" and "I needed to find out if this was a place I could unload" etc. I brought her back to tonight's session and asked her what she wanted to know from the group. After some difficulty [she likes to tell stories] I got her to frame her questions:

"Did I overwhelm and scare you?" and "How do you feel about my being a group member?" Predictably the group gave her very positive and appreciative feedback for being so honest and brave; several picked up their logs from last week and read their comments, such as Kim's: "Donna has arrived and I felt pain & depth and sadness and all those *wonderful emotions* [italics mine] that are so hard to find". At this point I asked Donna to pay attention to her body since I noticed what appeared to me a softening and relaxing in her [*in individual sessions she often expressed tension in her eye and her neck and since I think one of the goals of treatment is to help people read and integrate their bodily actions and reactions I try to attend to these, recognizing change and growth is usual slow and incremental and needs much repetition*].

Later in the session I asked her now that she had learned that she wasn't overwhelming and scary where that left her, what else could she accomplish here. At first she didn't know then she said she wanted to find the "wild woman part of her". When I asked her if she could now get in touch with and express that part of herself she came up blank. So I asked her to close her eyes and "hear" a melody [*this often provides a clue*]. She heard and imaged a TV commercial in which a staid librarian fantasizes having her hair washed by three handsome men. That's as far as she went [*sounded pretty sexy to me yet she never mentioned sex so I let* it *be*]. Not content, though, with what she had already done, Donna asked if she could do a round telling each person how she felt about her/him. I said of course if no one has an objection. No one did so she proceeded, ranging from anger at Karl for falling asleep last time to a deep connection with Kim.

She then brought out a gift bag and gave it to Kim. It contained a mirror – a follow-up on the last session when Donna had encouraged Kim to look in the mirror in the morning and say nice things to herself [*ordinarily Kim says nasty things to herself.]* I asked the group for feedback to Donna. Both Tonya and Camilla expressed amazement at how quickly Donna had jumped into the group. Tonya [*who obviously had kept count]* said

"This is only your fifth session and today you started the session – and you did a round. It took me years to do a round"; and Kim added "And I don't think I've done one yet in four years" [*I know enough about Kim to let that stand alone without pushing her further by saying something like "Well...?What about now?"*]

In her log Donna wrote "Feeling more comfortable...I hope I can continue to be honest...I liked being the center of attention last week – for so long I've been a cookie cutter type. I needed the attention". [*So she's hooked and I think this will be very good for her. She's already becoming one of my favorites – so I'd better be careful*].

Some rounds and risks

The session lagged at this point. A lot had already happened. A member had left and a member had 'arrived'. I suggested each person consider what was happening for her/him. Camilla, who has taken to Donna, said she saw sadness in Donna's face when she had spoken of love in the previous session. Donna acknowledged this and Camilla said maybe she – Donna – was fearful of opening up her heart. I asked Camilla if she resonated to this. She said she did. I asked her if she would be willing to do a round in which she told each person what she experienced in her heart with regard to that person. She agreed. I suggested she place her hand over her heart and let it talk to her; after some fluster and anxiety she proceeded to do it. To Donna and Nancy her heart said "I feel connected and warm to you". To Karl and Kim she owned that though she liked them she didn't really 'know' them and didn't feel deeply connected. "What about Jack I asked. After some hesitation she said to him "I'm very afraid of you. You're so big and at times so loud". "And what about me?" I asked. She looked directly at me and softly said "I love you". [*though this might be a mild experiment to some, for Camilla it was very difficult, very intense and very important*].

The rest of the session was devoted to work by Jason and then Jack, the latter being initiated by Kim asking him if he was okay. He said "No" and gradually exposed his shame over his emotional "hunger". Haltingly and very painfully he expressed his hopelessness and his sense that "I am dying day by day". [*He is of course by pulling into himself*]. Sympathetic efforts by the group were to no avail at enabling him to do more at this time. [*It was a small step though*]

We close tensely

Jack followed with only a few minutes left. His work was not sympathy-arousing. He turned to Kim and spewed at her viciously, accusing her of being disrespectful toward him and taking Amy's side over a scheduling issue. [*This referred to a former member who had requested a change in our schedule from meeting Tuesdays to Mondays, due to an unavoidable situation at work. Everyone but Jack had said no problem. Jack refused on vague grounds that smacked of vindictiveness. Kim, who was quite friendly with Amy, had been quite angry at Jack and let him know it*]. The group, including me, was stunned at this outburst, both because of its coming as it did months after the event and because of its viciousness. Our time was up and I stuck to the structure, urging that we revisit this next time.

At this point the group members filled out their logs [see Appendix A] and left.

Chapter 2 – Historical Considerations

Group therapy had been practiced for about 15 years before gestalt Therapy made its formal debut in 1951 with the 'bible' by Perls, Hefferline and Goodman. In particular, psycho-analysts, notably Slavson (1970) developed and promoted the use of groups in treatment. A few years before the publication of PHG, Fritz and Laura Perls had begun together to offer individual psychotherapy and to teach and proselytize their new approach in groups in their apartment in NYC. These groups came to be called training groups, though they were primarily therapeutic rather than didactic in nature. That is to say the focus was more experiential than cognitive/theoretical.

In the late 1950's, Fritz Perls left NYC and promoted gestalt Therapy in various parts of the country, famously at Esalen in Monterey, California. He ran workshops over extended time periods – weekends and weeklong for instance – and worked mainly with one individual at a time in the presence of the rest of the group. He called this *group therapy*, though it doesn't meet the standards of many, including me, to merit the term.

It didn't qualify as group, since there was little or no attention to group process nor was the full group included in the individual hot seat work. And also it was questionably therapy; first, there was not any particular intent to work with a given individual over time, though probably many people came back often. For another, the membership of the groups was always changing, preventing working through of complex relationship issues, except perhaps with the leader. And the lack of continuity worked against a participant risking repetitively – and without repetition there is little durable change, if any. All in all, as leader, Fritz was not interested in being responsible for participants' growth over time, only their experience during the duration of the workshops. For these reasons I don't consider his efforts group therapy; rather they are better characterized as workshops and demonstrations [he did many demonstrations of gestalt work to professionals at hospitals and clinics and wherever he was invited]. This style of working and teaching, though not – again in my view – group therapy, was enormously important in the growth and spread of gestalt Therapy. And I do not want to minimize the impact his work had on many people, some of whom I know. My focus here is on group therapy, as I view it. It also needs saying that at the same time, Fritz's methods had the deleterious effect of contributing to gestalt Therapy as being seen as irresponsible, out of control and simplistic –particularly when people with very little training set themselves up as gestalt therapists. It took a long time for gestalt therapy to evolve into the judicious and responsible treatment modality it is today.

At the same time, Laura Perls remained in NYC and continued to train and treat people in her groups, while also being the central force in the development of the NY Institute for Gestalt Therapy, the first Gestalt Therapy institute. Al though she also offered demonstrations and training in other places, she provided her clients in NY an ongoing continuous experience with essentially a stability of membership in the groups, justifying the characterization of her work as 'group therapy'. Both she and Fritz paid little attention to group dynamics, though, and worked primarily using the 'hot seat' model in which the therapist works with one individual as the group silently witnessed. The term 'hot seat' referred to an empty chair next to Fritz's; he invited participants to leave their seats and sit in the designated seat next to his, and to work with him. I never saw Laura Perls work this way; whoever in the group wanted to work stayed put for the work – unless of course the work required movement, which it often did. For the most part, she worked with one individual with the group as audience, essentially 'hot seat' work without a 'designated' hot seat.

As stated above, then, neither Fritz nor Laura paid much attention to group dynamics. If someone was missing or dropped out, it was not paid attention to. Endings were not emphasized, nor were intra-group tensions or group-as-a-whole themes. For instance in Laura's groups, at times a visitor from Israel or somewhere would drop in for a session or two and then disappear. The group was neither consulted prior nor considered after.

This is not the place to go into detail about group dynamics. Here, though, are the main concerns involved [tack on 'in a group' to each item]:

- leadership styles and their effects
- membership
- cohesion
- pressures from other members
- rules and norms
- goals and tasks
- phases
- the dynamics of power
- the effects of the group on the individual.

For a good overview see Cartwright and Zander [1956]

Some gestalt theorists are currently exploring the tantalizing question "Does the group have a self?" That, however, is still in its early stage.

By the mid -1970's, then, some of us were noticing this deficiency and exploring ways to integrate group dynamics into gestalt group therapy. One night as Ruth Ronall and I were driving up Sixth Ave after a NY Institute meeting, Ruth in her playful way composed a limerick about this state of affairs which went something like this:

Once Ruth Ronall said to Bud Feder
[pronounced 'feeder']
You know I'm an inveterate reader.
Yet I've never read a gestalt book
Which takes a good look
At dynamics among members plus leader

This got us going and soon we were making plans for the first somewhat comprehensive book on Gestalt Group Therapy, namely <u>Beyond the Hot Seat: Gestalt Approaches to Group,</u> which was published in 1980. As editors of the book we sought out others who had been thinking along the same lines, particularly from the Cleveland Gestalt Institute. Two of the outstanding group practitioners from Cleveland – Elaine Kepner and Joseph Zinker – accepted our invitation, and soon we had a full complement of contributors who wrote about therapy groups, marathon groups, classroom groups, organizational groups and groups with special populations.

All in all it is a good book and is still to this day the only book I know of which is totally devoted to the gestalt approach to groups. Even though the book is somewhat uneven it had an enormous influence by educating many therapists to the possibilities within gestalt group work for other than hot seat work and for broad applications, as in the classroom. The book didn't invent these theories or applications – it brought them together and spread the word on them.

In 1974 I compiled a survey of gestalt group work in the U.S. and found that 31% of practitioners employed only hot seat work. When Jon Frew did a similar study in 1988, eight years after *Beyond the Hot Seat*, this percentage had dropped to 16%. He and I surveyed again in 2002 and the percentage remained about the same.

So whereas originally, all gestalt group work was with the hot seat model, today only about 1 in 5 practitioners work this way. The others employ either interpersonal work, or a group-as-a whole or systems focus or a combination of two or more of the models mentioned above.

Graphically:

Approach	1988	2002
Hot Seat	16%	19%
Interpersonal	19%	24%
Systems Focus	4%	3%
Two or all of above	61%	54%

As Schoenberg and I wrote [2005], the models other than hot seat mentioned above are characterized by "real relationships between members, peer dialogue, a broader range of present-centered experience, a sense of the group-as-a-whole, emphasis on intimate contact among members to create acceptance and support for experiment and risk" [ibid, p. 222].

Another way to put this, as Frew does in a comment on the same chapter, is that the gestalt therapy core principle of 'field theory' "embraces the dance of dependence and independence, the perennial polarity that bounds and defines interdependence." He goes

38

on to say that hot seat work, on the other hand, moves the client towards "internal autonomous support and away from group support" [ibid, p. 222].

To take advantage of the rich potential of the group, practitioners such as Kepner [1980] emphasized that there are different levels of work possible in a group. There is the individual or intrapersonal level in which the therapist helps a member in self-exploration. There is the interpersonal level in which the work is between two or more people present, including the leader. And there is the work with the group-as-a whole, exploring themes common to all during which the focus is not any specific member or dyad or triad.

In Kepner's language the group leader is essentially the 'manager' of the group rather than the 'director', a label which aptly describes the hot seat leader. Since most of the time the opportunity for working at any one of these levels is present, the 'manager' guides the group to the level she believes would be most fruitful and appropriate at the moment.

For example, looking at our sample session, the group begins on an intrapersonal level focusing on Walt and his desire to leave the group. I shifted this to an interpersonal level, asking the group to give feedback. Continuing in this mode, Walt initiated an interpersonal round, telling how he felt about each person. When he said to me "I don't trust you" I attempted to work dyadically with him [just him and me], however he refused...and left for good.

This was an opportunity for me to initiate some group-as-a-whole work; for instance I brought in the theme of being left and explored how the group was resonating to this; or I could have asked how this group felt right now in its new configuration, eight of us instead of nine, fewer men members than women, etc. After that we turned to some intrapersonal work as Donna erupted with her fears and projections and this was followed by interpersonal exchanges and rounds.

Before going on to the main thrust of the book – practical guidance – we have two more didactic chapters as we turn to the question "So What is Gestalt Group Therapy?"

Chapter 3 – What is Gestalt Group Therapy?

Gestalt Therapy and other approaches

Since many schools of psychotherapy utilize groups, what qualifies a group as a gestalt group? Actually sometimes it is hard to know, in that a therapist who calls himself a 'modern analyst' or a 'humanistic therapist' or an 'existential therapist' may run his group in a way indistinguishable from a gestalt therapy group. This might be due to several things:

 *the practitioner from another school may have absorbed much of what gestalt therapy introduced into the world of psychotherapy with or without being aware of it. Much of what we have contributed has been integrated into current psychotherapy without it being attributed to gestalt therapy *another reason is that some schools of psychotherapy have a similar perspective yet practice in a less holistic way. For example, a number of years ago I taught a course in Abnormal Psychology to undergraduates and I used a book by the psychiatrist Harry Stack Sullivan who branched off from Freud and developed the analytic school known as Interpersonal Relations. I had read Sullivan as an undergraduate myself and liked his attitude. He worked a lot with schizophrenics and I was very pleased with his statement "We [*he meant therapists and everybody else*] are more like schizophrenics than we are different".

When I read his book [Conceptions of Modern Psychiatry [1945] in preparation for my course, I was amazed at how similar many of its principles are to gestalt therapy, although expressed more formally. I refer to the focus on dialogue, contact, I-thou interaction, respect for differences, etc. Yet a Sullivanian would never consider himself a gestaltist, despite the many similarities – and of course there are differences too. My point is an observer of a Sullivanian group might think it was gestalt group. However it would be lacking the breadth of gestalt therapy groups as I will point out.

The Essentials of Gestalt Group Therapy

In gestalt Therapy group work, we would find the following principles incorporated into the practice, though of course the emphasis and inclusion vary from therapist to therapist:

- field theory
- dialogue
- viewing the group, not only the individuals in it, as
- an organism, or at least a force
- group dynamic elements, such as rules, norms, goals,
- etc
- organismic self-regulation
- contact and contact-interruptions, both individual
- and group-as-a-whole
- balancing self-support and support from others
- present-centeredness [here and now]
- awareness, including body awareness
- experimentation/ risk-taking

43

- a holistic approach, including openness to all manner
- of creative experiences, including music, art, movement, talking gibberish, etc

Regarding the above characteristics of a gestalt therapy group, all of these elements would not be found in any one group session nor would any one therapist be equipped or comfortable enough to encourage all of the above, particularly in the creative modes. As I once heard Laura Perls succinctly state "There are as many gestalt therapies as there are gestalt therapists". Yet unless a therapist adheres to the basic principles which can be simply and perhaps somewhat simplistically summarized as the three "'E's": existential, experiential and experimental [again thanks to Laura Perls, 1977], she is not practicing gestalt therapy; and unless she is simultaneously cognizant of and attentive to the principles relating to group listed above, the therapist is not practicing Gestalt <u>Group</u> Therapy. Put with a positive spin, a Gestalt Group Therapist applies both the basic gestalt therapy principles and the basic tenets of group dynamics.

Our Sample Session

Applying this to our sample session, the session actually begins with a risk, since Walt's usual way of dealing with dissatisfaction is to just break contact without dialogue. Of course if I hadn't met him in the market, this might not have happened. Now I don't say that this one piece of new behavior would lead to permanent change, yet at least it models healthier contact for him and for the group. And actually my dialoguing with him in the market is an example of good contact and being an *authentic* person. I refer to myself, for in the market I told him I was sorry he was leaving, I respected his decision and I'd appreciate his coming in to tell the group about it. Additionally I was applying a group rule, though bent. In the contract between us [see Appendix A] one item is that members give the group 4 week's notice before departing to allow for closure and working through. From a systems point of view I explored with the group the effect of Walt's departure on this system, this group, as we looked at and experienced the 'new' group. Regarding dialogue, throughout the session as leader I encouraged direct dialogue between and among members [some call this "I-

Thou" contact]; I also attempted this with Walt when he stated "I don't trust you", yet as you may recall he rejected the suggestion. In Donna's work, I moved her as quickly as I could from the past to the present. After she received feedback I attended to her bodily awareness. By speaking her piece she was developing *self-support* and by allowing the group to encourage her she was balancing this with improved dependence on others, taking a small step toward interdependence. Although this session did not feature the use of creative expression, I think the fantasy piece with Donna about a TV commercial qualifies in a small way. A year later, though one of the most memorable groups I've ever been part of was when Donna recapitulated her life for the group in the style of a performance artist and with numerous props and artifacts. I won't say I led this group, other than to say "Okay, let's start" and "It's time to stop". Donna took over completely * and nobody complained. It was fascinating and I wish it had been taped.

Other parts of the sample session can be joined to the principles enumerated above. I suggest before going on, take a few minutes and play with this.

Chapter 4 - Why Gestalt Group Therapy?

The title of this chapter reflects a question commonly asked of me by clients to whom I recommend joining a gestalt therapy group. Being a fairly quick learner, and realizing this will happen, I have prepared a fairly lengthy document [summarized in Appendix A] for these potential group members and ask them to take it home, read it so we can then discuss it.

Potential benefits of GGT

This document, about twelve pages long, goes into some detail singing the praises of GGT. Actually in my case as leader this document focuses more on interactive GGT which is the only kind I practice nowadays, with the exception of training groups or marathon groups. In those groups I often include some 'hot seat' work. Here, in brief, are the benefits which I discuss, under the general category of improvement in interpersonal relating and in more effective living. To say this more technically, in a group a member has excellent opportunities to dissolve fixed gestalten and replace them with new pattern [see Ch 5 for my "Model for Changing"]. Here are some of the benefits which I indicate a client may reasonably expect to receive from group participation:

- increased awareness of one's functioning in the present; this refers to awareness on all levels: bodily, cognitively, interpersonally
- learning by doing
- experimenting with new ways of interacting
- becoming more direct and clear
- becoming more comfortable with self-disclosure,
- become more comfortable with intimacy and sexuality
- learning better ways of resolving conflicts
- developing a better understanding of counterproductive patterns
- developing better communication skills
- getting helpful honest feedback from fellow members.

Of course, for some group members the opposite of some of the above may be true. For instance, the overly narcissistic person will hopefully learn more about swallowing needs than expressing them; he already is an expert at expressing them. Or the overly combative person may improve self-restraint rather than self-assertion.

The Bottom Line

The most important point is that through the group experiences, members will become more aware of fixed patterns, self-interruptions and other hindrances to more satisfying relating and living. Following these awarenesses, they will have opportunities to experiment and learn new 'better' patterns. And, as I frequently emphasize by both spoken and written word, usually a lot of repetition is necessary before old fixed or frozen patterns can be thawed out, dissolved and replaced by new more flexible ones.

Chapter 5. My Basic Model for Promoting Change through Gestalt Group Therapy

This chapter provides my basic thinking in what promotes changing with regard to others through participation in a group. Everything else flows from this. By this I mean everything else provides the ground for and leads up to the hard work a client must do to accomplish important changes in her ways of relating to others. These changes in her core being, so to speak, come about by virtue of risking, aka experimenting. For example, in the chapter in which I discuss the therapist [Ch 11], the importance of those ideas and suggestions is the part a therapist plays in providing the abovementioned ground. And similarly regarding the other aspects covered in this book: group composition, developing and maintaining the ground, etc – all are in the ultimate service of optimizing the client's likelihood of experimenting and risking, the essentials for significant changing interpersonally.

Now as I said in the previous chapter, a therapy group has many other benefits. I am speaking here only of those behaviors generally known as interpersonal.

This is not a highly theoretical booklet since I don't have a highly theoretical mind. What follows is about as theoretical as I get:

Trauma

Most core issues which cause difficulties in life are the result of trauma; by trauma I don't necessarily mean a major event; I also mean an aggregate of smaller events; these often take place in childhood yet may also occur later in life.

Creative Adjusting

The individual creatively adjusts in some way that helps her/him cope or survive or deal with the situation.

Fixed Gestalten

If the person utilizes this creative adjustment a great deal, s/he becomes very good, even expert at it and at the extreme does it automatically [out of awareness fully or partially]. This in

Gestalt terms is called a *fixed gestalt* [alternately a fixed pattern or a fixity –in German by the way the plural is 'gestalten'].

Contact Interruptions

When this adjustive behavior continues beyond the situation calling for it and particularly when it is out of awareness, the person uses it inappropriately and randomly, often to her/his disadvantage. The results include disturbances of contact and contact interruptions, such as confluence, deflection, introjection, isolation,etc.

[This counterproductive use of a fixed gestalt, when it occurs in contact with a therapist, is called 'transference' by some, a term from psychoanalysis which I don't like in gestalt Therapy, yet use it if you must. Similarly if the therapist responds with a fixed pattern of his own, some call this counter transference. We could also call it bad therapy, though good can be salvaged from it *see Kohut's *'transmutating internalization'* (Elson, 1986)].

Crises

If the fixed gestalt causes major problems in life and relationships, the person may experience distress, or be in crisis. It is often at this point that the individual enters therapy.

Awareness

Ideally, in the therapeutic situation, the client becomes aware [or perhaps more aware] of this fixed and counterproductive, often destructive, pattern. One of the beauties of group is that it provides a complex scenario of people and events to bounce off of – and get in trouble with in one way or another, heightening awareness in accessible clients.

Commitment to Changing and Risking

If awareness is followed by a desire and decision to change, the group situation offers multiple opportunities for experimenting and risking. In order for this to happen, the group must offer sufficient support for the anxiety that accompanies such risk-taking. A main job of the group therapist is to develop, nurture and maintain a sufficiently [not overly] supportive environment [see Ch 8], creating what we call the "safe emergency". If all these conditions are met, the client is on the road [the long road] to changing - dissolving old *fixed gestalten* [patterns] and creating new ones.

Repetition

In order for the new pattern to dominate the old one, the   client is encouraged to to risk and practice these new behaviors in daily life. In order for these new behaviors to 'take'   much repetition is required [nevertheless as Andras Angyal said:

> "to remain well, the client must recognize that his old patterns have not been erased once and for all …..though it is a bitter pill to swallow for a person who had hoped the golden era had come, one must learn that recovery means   no more   than this: the strength of the old problematic   pattern has been reduced as one has learned to live in a more wholesome fashion.   But the potentiality for one's special way of malfunctioning always remains alive when one succumbs to great stress and retreats into an angry or anxious state. This realization can help one deal with these relapses and resist the temptation to indulge in self-blame and a feeling of helplessness and final defeat" [1982, p.260].

An Example

Here is good example of the model from my own life: early on, in childhood, I developed the creative adjustment of lying, to_protect myself from harsh parental criticism and punishment [the trauma]. I got extremely skillful at it and developed it to an extreme point, in fact to the point that I began to do it automatically, and often with minimal or no awareness until after the fact. Though this served me well in my family of origin it was very harmful to my later relationships. Only through therapy, after becoming aware of this pattern and realizing that telling the truth and facing the situation was a much more wholesome way of living, did I begin to risk and experiment and to a large degree change my pattern. Yet, as Angyal wisely said, the potential for the old pattern is always there and I require much vigilance to resist it ...and of course I'm not always successful [and that's the truth!].

Our sample Session

One simple example from our sample session is Walt's risking coming into the session and confronting the group rather than avoiding this confrontation. From individual work with Walt I had learned that his father was a very harsh disciplinarian [the trauma] and Walt's creative adjustment was to avoid confrontation with him. This becomes his *modus vivendi,* his fixed gestalt. So confronting the group was an experiment [a risk] for him. By assuring him that I would see to it that the group did not pressure him to stay I apparently gave him enough support to do this -- even though he didn't trust me fully. Unfortunately as previously mentioned he didn't feel supported enough to go further on this issue with me...and whether he took this courageous act [confronting] into his daily life I was not privileged to know.

The reader is invited to review the sample session and see if other examples of this model emerge.

Chapter 6.
Creating an Ongoing
Gestalt Therapy Group

Unfortunately it ain't so easy no mo'. In the late 1970's, when I came into my own as a gestalt group therapist in NJ, it was common for me to have four or five weekly groups. I remember for instance, one period when I had two adult mixed groups on weeknights, another on Saturday morning, a 'housewives' group midday during the week and an adolescent group after school one weekday. On top of that I had one training group one weeknight and a marathon group about one weekend a month.

People wanted group [except for the adolescents of course who needed some prodding].

This gradually changed after about 1985 or '90. I still maintained a training group yet slowly the number of adult groups shrunk to one [and I was too old for an adolescent group even if I could have developed one]. The burst of interest in community and openness that characterized the wonderful 1960's and 70's slowly dissolved as our society reverted to the conservatism and to the conformity that was so pronounced through into the 60's. And the groups that have evolved and prospered since 1990 have been conservative, conformist groups in religious circles. I am generalizing of course, yet generalities are based in realties.

Nevertheless group therapy still exists, or else I wouldn't be writing this. Managed care loves it because it is cheaper. Community hospitals with psychiatric wards do a great deal of group work with their patients, because they are not staffed for individual work. The nature of these groups, because of the fragility of the group members and the acute states they are in, is much more structured and directed than the groups within private practice or even outpatient clinics * at least that is my experience in those settings, and I've worked in all three.

In this chapter I am going to provide some guidelines for star- ting a group with 'outpatients' [I dislike the term, yet 'out- clients' doesn't work either]. In other words, starting a group in private practice or a community mental health clinic or possibly on a college campus (though I hear those aren't very popular anymore either).

There are two main ways of developing a pool of candidates for your new group: by recommending it to your own clients in individual therapy and by soliciting or being offered members from colleagues. Also, in some communities, for instance in Berkeley where I am living at the moment, there is an unusually eclectic psychotherapy institute with over four hundred members who practice a wide variety of treatment modalities, i.e. cognitive, behavioral, 'psychodynamic' [although I thought all good psychological treatment was dynamic], a little gestalt, etc. In its directory and its mailing the institute lists groups being led – all types: gay, straight, men's, women's, smokers, and on and on. In this town I have also seen groups advertised on bulletin boards outside of grocery stores and in the many New Age papers distributed at restaurants. However, this is Berkeley. It is hardly typical yet my point is that one can be creative in seeking group members.

Whether buying ads in papers pays off I don't know – yet they do it so I suppose it must.

Leaving that aside, I imagine [having no data] that most groups evolve from the practices of the leader[s]. The therapist typically receives a phone call, from someone who is looking for individual therapy or couples therapy or help with a child. Assuming the therapy goes forward, at some point it may be appropriate – and acceptable to the client, or one of them or both if it is a couple * to suggest that he or they consider joining a group. This requires good tact and good timing and good reasons.

Some will be willing to consider this, others not. In the former case I like to be prepared with some literature which the client can take home, read and bring back for further discussion [see Appendix A].

The reasons for recommending group therapy vary with the individual. Fritz Perls was wont to say that therapy could fill the holes in the personality. In a similar vein, group therapy can provide particular and pointed growth and change in certain areas of weakness which the person manifests. The secret person can learn to be more open, the timid one to be more assertive, the avoidant one to be more *contactful*, and so forth. By this point in the person's treatment, both of you are no doubt aware of the holes in this client's personality. This doesn't meant that there will be no other benefits, yet honing in on one or more core deficits or problematic aspects of the individual's being will be very helpful in selling the group modality. Unfortunately nowadays it often needs selling. I rarely get calls requesting group unless this has been specifically recommended by the client's individual therapist.

In the latter case, it usually leads to some contact with the individual therapist. Whether this is occasional or more often depends on the situation as well as relationship between you and her. Of course a signed release is technically required and a good idea.

Obviously it makes a big difference if one is starting a group from scratch or making an addition or replacement to an ongoing group. The former requires a pretty large pool to draw on in most cases, which is hard for the new therapist to come by. So it may take a while before you can have a group in private practice. The latter [adding a member] has some tricky aspects to it. These include:

*Democracy: in my view once a group has started, it is no longer *my* group it is *our* group. I am an equal among equals, though we have different roles. So any change in structure, style, numbers, schedule, etc is now a group decision. Referring back to adding a member, when I want to do so, I bring it up in the group and we decide about it as a group. I operate on the principle of unanimity; all members must agree to the addition. It could be that a member's refusal to add a member is grist for the therapeutic mill, so I might suggest we explore the matter, yet that doesn't give me permission to override the member. In actuality, no group of mine has ever refused in principle to add a member when one has left. Some have objected with regard to the timing.

*Timing: at times a particular group is in the midst of some hot work. This might be conflictual work, i.e. two or three or all members are engaged in some important controversy. Or it might be harmonious thematic work, having to do, say, with some important existential issue such as sex or loss or mortality. A new member usually changes and interrupts the focus for a month or two as the new member must be assimilated and adjusted to. Ordinarily I tell the group I have a candidate and encourage questions and reactions. I am quite sensitive to this as it wasn't done in Laura Perls' groups, to my dissatisfaction. If my timing is off and I am obtuse enough to suggest a new member inappropriately, usually objections are raised and I get the point. Even though I am usually astute enough to be better attuned than that, yet I have been known to screw up, as we all do. Given enough time the group will work through or get past its objections and then the new member can be introduced

*Previous connections: it may be, especially in smaller communities, that a proposed member may be acquainted with a veteran member. If this is so, I give the veteran member the prerogative of deciding whether it is okay for the friend or acquaintance to join. Of course, this isn't necessary when a veteran member initiates the proposal for her friend to join. And I have no objection to that. I myself was in group with two

friends – and it strengthened our relationships. As a matter of fact, many therapists belong to 'peer' groups to work on their own stuff [as well as to get peer supervision] and these often include dyads or triads of friends.

*Couples: a related issue concerns couples in the same group. This is more complicated and needs to be evaluated based on each particular couple. When I do agree to a couple being in the same group [whether they join together or one comes in later] I do it on the condition they do not do work on their couple's relationship in this group -- that if they need to do that, do it in a couples' group or in separate marital/couples therapy.

Otherwise the group can get bogged down on their couples stuff. Putting it another way, they must agree to operate as individuals in the group. This doesn't mean they can't interact with each other in the group, yet they must do it on the basis of their here-and-now experience, not their out-side experiences. There is a fine line here, and pretty tricky, especially for the novice therapist. A variation on this theme is when two people in the same group become a couple after having met in the group. Actually I can recall at least three such happenings with all three couple eventually marrying – and still together. If this occurs, then the approach described above applies – at least in my groups.

Although what I've just written refers more to later developments than to starting a group, I include it now since in one sense any change in membership means that now we are starting a new group.

When considering inviting clients to join a group. Keep in mind the following considerations:

*Size: For years I have recommended that the ideal size for an ongoing weekly group is eight. This is large enough to provide a wide variety of interpersonal dynamics and core issues to emerge. It is small enough to allow ample attention to each member. And it is large enough to cope with the inevitable absences. In the northeast where I practiced, in winter there were frequent illnesses and interference of ice, fog and snow. In summer there are vacations. So, all in all it is a cause for celebration if all eight members are present two or three weeks in a row. To my satisfaction, I recently came across a theory by a sociologist [Ike, 1987] which supports this. According to Ike, the human being has a limited fund of 'sympathy' due to being raised evolutionarily in families usually of no more than nine. Therefore he warns against groups being larger than 9 when 'sympathy' is an important ingredient in the success of that group, as in group therapy. So, smugly, I declare him to be right – as I knew all along. For marathon groups though I like 12-14 participants to keep the energy flowing over a long stretch of time, such as a weekend. Other kinds of groups may have different 'ideal' numbers, and probably each therapist has his own take on this.

*Gender balance: generally I strive for an approximation of gender balance in my groups, unless they are designed differently; I once had a men's group for a year, etc. Having an exact gender balance is of course not always possible and isn't critical.

*Personality balance: a group needs some live wires, so a group of all passive; inhibited; shy; constricted people is a very tough row to hoe * unless it's a theme-centered group and that is the theme. And a group with more than one borderline person will probably drown in lability, inconsistency, self-righteousness and projection [blaming].

*The first session: the beginning of the first group [and also the beginning a marathon, the first module] is very special. Unlike some therapists I don't start every group with a check-in round, yet I definitely would do something like that in the very first session or module. Starting a group is probably anxiety-producing for all at the least and terrifying to some. I suggest a significant amount of support in the first session for several reasons:

1 without it there's a lot of performance-anxiety work which I don't consider valuable; I'd much rather bypass it if possible. If it is core for some members, it will come up soon enough and can be attended to.

2 one of the main jobs of the therapist is to create a "safe enough' ground for scary work. By 'safe-enough' I mean a developing a balance between support and frustration: supportive enough to enable the client to work and frustrating enough so he is aware of his issues, feels them and sees the need to work on them.

Two references here are: [1] the chapter entitled "Here Comes the Neurotic" [a demeaning title in my view] in Fritz Perls book The Gestalt Approach (1973) and [2] the chapter entitled "Safety and Danger in the Gestalt Therapy Group" by me in Beyond the Hot Seat (1980; 2000).

I often start a first session informally, inviting the participants to come 15 or 30 minutes early for bagels or whatever. At one time, when I had a very large office, I had a spread of crackers and cheese and fruit with hot water for tea or instant coffee on a table at one end of the room. Members could partake not only before the session but throughout and after it. Laura Perls' groups met in her apartment and often I would be the first arrival.

The door was unlocked and she typically was playing Bach on the piano as I let myself in. Coffee and cookies were sitting on the nearby buffet. So through these provisions as well as her friendly nature, a great deal of support was provided. Nevertheless I was scared shitless my first session and I still remember parts of it vividly. Summing this aspect up, I recommend each therapist find her own way of providing necessary support in the context of this demanding situation. For every group, though, it is very important that the physical group be at least minimally adequate: this includes privacy, comfortable seating, accessible toilet facilities, facial tissues, etc. Obviously these do not guarantee good therapy, yet they provide part of the initial ground for the work.

Now I will take a look and see how these above conditions and suggestions apply to our sample session:

*Sources: all eight members were drawn from my individual therapy practice except for Jack, and he too indirectly came from my individual therapy practice. That is, he was referred for group by his girlfriend with whom he lived and she was an individual client of mine who was also in the group. After interviewing him, I was charmed into making the mistake of taking him on and into the group. I lived to regret both, since after a long honeymoon period in which I was idolized by him, I later became demonized by him. Actually this demonization came to a head out of the conflict he raised at the very end of the sample session. I'll say more about this later.

*Additions: in the sample session one member left. This meant that there was now one open spot in the group for an addition. In looking for a replacement, I had several criteria. One was for a man to keep the *gender balance*. Another was for a *lively self-energized* person since there were already some very shy timid self-interrupting members and Walt was, as mentioned, a live wire. On the exclusionary side, I was well-aware by this time that Jack was an explosive borderline person [there had been previous eruptions and once he put his fist through my wall] so I was clear I would not suggest another such. So ideally I was looking for an energetic, reasonable, balanced man. However, not immediately since the group was in a very hot place, which was going to get hotter. The timing was certainly not right for an addition – and wouldn't be for quite a while. So for now the size of the group would not match my ideal of eight members. When I did think the time was right and did have a suitable candidate, I would then propose him to the extant group [Jack left also after a protracted period of rigid paranoid inexorable irreconcilable disturbing disruptive memorable conflict*-obviously I have strong feelings about this].

As stated, Jack and his girlfriend Sally had a previous connection when he entered the group, which was about several years prior to the sample session. I made it clear before he came in that the "no couples work in group" rule applied, other than work in the group context. This they complied with fully. Another member of this group, Jason, had been in group for a very long time. Early on he met Trudy; they are one of the three couples alluded to earlier who developed a relationship through their group connection and married. While they were in group together [Trudy had left group a while ago] they complied with the rule and obtained couples' therapy when needed with a friend of mine. I haven't found violations of this rule to be a problem.

Chapter 7. The First Session

There is only one first session for a group and it has its own special features. As I mentioned last chapter, I do some things in this session which I usually don't do in other sessions, though there are exceptions [which will be mentioned as they come up]. Before I get to that, I want to repeat that preparation for the session is very desirable. This includes the aforementioned literature regarding the nature of this group, i.e. describing the type of group you will be leading: hot seat, interactive, systems, or a combination. You might also consider a contract similar to the one in Appendix A as well as any other literature or paperwork you deem necessary [such as a release form to a member's individual therapist] or desirable [such as readings].`

So now on to the actual first session, preparation is behind us. As I've said I often invite members to come a little early and have some snacks and beverages and to informally meet. When this designated time is over I call the session to order. This is a good time to say that I personally am generally a stickler for keeping to the schedule, not necessarily to the exact minute, yet pretty close. Yet at the first session I have a variation on this. Let's say tonight's meeting is scheduled to start at 7:45 and end at 9:30. I have invited members to arrive anytime after 7:30 and have let them know that snacks would be provided. At 7:45, regardless of the number of members present, I will say something like "OK, it's time to start. Please take a seat". In the event that some members are missing, I will then say "It's up to the group whether we start right now or make an exception at this first meeting and wait a few more minutes for latecomers. Let's talk about it". If there is not unanimous agreement to wait a bit, then I will start. I don't go by majority in this kind of situation, since we have a contract. Unless everyone wants to modify it, I stick with it. Usually nobody objects to waiting ten minutes or so. I do this in extended groups too at the first module, be it a training group or a marathon. I do not offer this option after the first session of an ongoing group or at subsequent modules in extended groups. At the appointed time I start with whoever is present.

At the first session or module it is important to review group rules and clarify them if requested. Here are my rules for groups:

*no physical violence; violation may be cause for termination of the violator [I've never had to eject anyone for this though I've had to enforce the rule in the instance of minor unwanted physical contact]

*confidentiality: members are free to discuss their own process with nonmembers yet it is incumbent on them to protect the identity and process of other members

*contact outside of group: it is up to members whether or not they want to have contact with any other member[s] outside of group, recognizing that anything of significance which takes place between or among members is grist for the mill during sessions. Imposing secrecy on another member is against the rules.

*notification of absence: should a member need to miss a session she is responsible to let the group know, by notifying me or another member who will be in attendance. This also applies with regard to serious lateness.

*interactive focus: if it is one of my interactive groups, the rule is that members may only bring up issues or events which are directly related to this group. Their concerns about their jobs, their relationships, their finances, etc.

*while important issues are off limits during an interactive group. It is their responsibility to find other resources for getting help with such concerns.

Since I ask members to fill out a log [see Appendix A] after each session, this needs some clarifying. The way it works is I have a clipboard for each member and on the back of it is a label with the member's first name clearly marked. When members arrive for a session all the clipboards are lying face down on the floor, names showing. Each member picks up his log and is able to see what he wrote last time and any comments I have made. Of course not all bother to read these at the beginning. It is up to them, just as it is up to them whether or not they fill them out after each session, which usually takes about five minutes at most. Naturally at the first session the board has a blank log form on it. It may surprise you yet my clients are very enamored of these logs and rarely skip filling one out. Perhaps this is because it gives each person a chance to have a small private exchange with me.

During this initial phase of the initial session I welcome any other inquiries of an informational or logistic nature. Usually by now most of them have been covered, and I suggest a round asking each member to identify herself by name, tell us what she is aware of including thoughts, feelings and bodily sensations and to tell us what she wants to get out of this experience. I ask each person to do this within five minutes or less and I ask other members to ask no questions. By the end of this we are about halfway through the session. I may ask "Any PS's?" There may or may not be. Then there is often a pause and for the first time the member faces the fertile void. Who will be brave enough to start? Or who will be too anxious to keep still? And other possibilities. The fascinating process unfolds.

Some therapists may utilize exercises at this juncture. I prefer not to. To me this is too much structure and order and support. I think I've given enough support so far. Now I want to see the chaos out of which order emerges. I also do a couple of things which are probably not too common [I really don't know]. Let's say the group's time is from 7:45-9:30 pm. I do the following:

>at 7:45 I put up a sign outside my office reading "Group in Session – Members Please Enter". By this time I have read the logs [other than Session One of course] and made any comments I want on them, such as "Can you risk telling the group what you just told me?" and the clipboards are on the floor. For the next ten minutes members who arrive may 'schmooze" [socialize]. I am usually in the room, though occasionally I am doing something else for a few minutes somewhere else. I participate in whatever way I feel like that particular evening. We may talk weather, politics, sports, family, job, cars, movies, whatever. I don't lead and I don't therapize. This module emerged at the suggestion of a member who complained she wanted to know more about other members not

80

just the problematic stuff that comes up in sessions. We tried this and liked it.

>at 7:55 I ring a little gong and ask everyone to be still for five minutes and pay attention to the breath and get centered. I have, by the way, turned the sign over outside and it now reads "Meditation in Progess -- Please Wait". I don't want latecomers coming in during this.

>at 8:00 I tap the gong once, a signal for members to give some thought for one minute to what they want to accomplish tonight

>at 8:01 I tap the gong twice, ending the silent period. I open the door, admitting latecomers and if not everyone has arrived turn the sign back to "Group in Progress – Members Please Enter". The work begins.

>at 9:30 I indicate the session is over. This can be in various ways. For instance, at the end of the sample session [Ch. 2] I suggested that we come back next time to the angry interaction which had just emerged. At other times I may simply say "Time to stop" or I may make a group-as-a-whole comment, such as "It seemed to me

that the group was intent on avoiding risking tonight – I'm interested to see if that's true next week too". The possibilities are endless of course depending on how the session has gone – which one never knows in advance. Generally I try to stop as close to 9:30 as possible, and this is usually doable....and the group gets the idea pretty quickly.

For the next five minutes or so members are filling out their logs and handing them to me, and leaving with or without a hug depending on the member.

Chapter 8 The Ground for Changing

As perhaps I didn't emphasize enough in Ch 5 [My Basic Model for Changing], the hard sweaty work that results in changing is done by the client. In gestalt terms this is 'Risking or Experimenting' followed by 'Repeating or Rehearsing'. It is the leader's job, much easier, to create and maintain the ground for this process, and this applies to group therapy just as well as it does to all forms of therapy * individual, couples, family, etc [if there are any other]. I said easier – not easy.

As I see it, this is a lot of what we do as therapists, initially creating this ground and then maintaining it. Fortunately the nuances are many and the challenges ever present, so the fascination remains. And the rewards, besides financial and prestigious, are so satisfying, as one sees many individuals changing and growing and developing a more satisfying life.

With regard to group therapy, here are some essentials -- some of which have already been spoken of in this opus * which are relevant to this topic:

*the therapist: "no doubt the single most important variable affecting the group's sense of safety is the person of the therapist" [Feder, 1980, p. 46]. This of course can't be taught other than mechanistically, since warmth, interest and maturity must either be there or evolve, as the case may be. Nevertheless good supervision and personal therapy can help this process; in particular personal experience as a group therapy member is very helpful for the empathic process. A tricky piece here is what we might call the leader's "mood"; that is, how the leader feels this day: tired, content, lazy, energetic, depressed, etc. This in part relates to self-revelation, though it can come through without intent too. More on this later [Ch 12].

*the balance between safety and danger: the group needs to be experienced as safe enough for risking and experimenting, while frustrating enough to bring contact disturbances to awareness. In other words it is not helpful if a group is too cozy or too confluent and if the therapist allows it to be too unchallenging and too undemanding. Again it is the balance that is essential. A member is unlikely to do good work if the group is perceived as either too safe or too dangerous.

*the selection of members: choosing members who will hopefully fit together in such a way as to provide an energetic, interesting, challenging and safe-enough ground

*the preparation of prospective members: providing them with enough grounding fore-contact so that they are ready to make maximum use of the GGT opportunity

*special attention during the first session to include all members: I probably do more rounds in a first session than any other, and frequently avoid extended work with one person, focusing more on the group as a whole and <u>all</u> the members

*the attention to the physical details: comfortable, or at least adequate seating;

privacy; lighting; toilet facilities; a supply of facial tissues, etc.

*knowing which decisions are best left to the group democratically and which are important to hold onto as leader [such as when to end the session]

*being very consistent, though not rigid, with rules and schedules

*utilizing self-revelation judiciously [see Ch 12]: balancing the inclusion of yourself in the work and self-revelation [being an equal member] with at certain times being outside the work [being the more objective or active therapist]; and also blending the two into the same moment, which for the therapist is quite satisfying

*clarifying any preexisting relationships, so that all members know "who knows whom and how?" as Ruth Ronall would to ask

*paying particular attention to characteristically shy members, giving them "as much support as necessary and as little as possible" – one of

Laura Perls' rules of thumb, which applies not only to this situation but to all situations in the therapeutic process. With the shy person the attention must be calibrated so as to encourage participation while not coming across as arm-twisting or shaming. Sometimes I make a deal with a client that I will bring him in at least once a session or bring up a topic he is particularly concerned about. Again this must be a mutually-agreed on arrangement, not a coercive or shaming one.

*attention to changes: anytime there is a change which affects the group, it is important to give ample time to exploring how this is for the members. This includes such events as: departure of a member, arrival of a new member, change of schedule, change of location and of course termination of a group. Recently I moved from the east coast to the west and for the four months before I left, much of the group's focus was on our ending. With regard to the change due to a new member, according to my clients it takes two months for the group to get back to where it was [and they should know], so the fewer such changes the better. This is a generalization, of course, and in the case of a new member who is abrasive or contrary or psychologically 'dumb' it could take longer, and for the psychologically ready and willing. It may only take one session.

*co-leadership: this is somewhat complicated so I will defer discussing this now; please refer to chapter 14.

Applying the above list to our sample session, first of course was the event of Walt's leaving. We processed this to some extent this meeting, yet I expect it will come up again in future ones and if it doesn't I will ask about it. With regard to self-revelation, I told the group of my regrets and sorrow about Walt's leaving...and allowed myself a sigh. Balancing support and frustration, the work with Donna involving her 'wild woman' fantasy is an example. I moved her along some with my suggestion for hearing a melody in her head, yet I passed on my notion that this sounded sexy, believing this would be pushing her too hard...this of course is a judgment call and there's no way I can know for sure that it was the right decision. Right or wrong, my point is that it was made on the basis of my concern about balancing these factors [support and pushing]. Pushing too hard, especially too early erodes the ground. I also was careful not to react in any way that she might perceive me as being disappointed or shaming her. Remember, shaming in a group is much more devastating than in an individual session, bad as that is.

Regarding consistency, note that I ended the session on time even though a heated exchange had just taken place. We could have been there a long time if we stayed with that, yet I didn't feel it was absolutely necessary to do so and I wasn't willing to sacrifice the image of myself as consistent which I had been careful to develop. Only an all-out crisis might persuade me to do otherwise - again that is a judgment call. I might also mention that we started on time and followed our beginning pattern [schmoozing, meditating] precisely. Other aspects from the above list can't be seen directly in this session. I refer to member selection, preparation of members and democratic decision-making. Looking into the future though, if I followed my own precepts I would look for a male member to provide gender balance, avoid bringing in another Jack [abrasive and harsh], seek someone with Walt's kind of energy and give the group ample time to decide when was a good time for the person to start once I had found him. At the same time I would stand firm that the group size is eight and that I would work towards reestablishing it as eight.

I mentioned earlier that I recently moved coast-to-coast. That meant I ended a training group, too – actually I stopped being its leader; it has continued without me as a peer group. What I'm getting at is that after I told the group I was leaving, it was the group's decision to be closed to new members for the five months until I left, even though we had openings.

In the next chapter I will talk about maintaining the ground that has been established, recognizing that this is a bit of an artificial distinction.

Chapter 9. Maintaining the
Ground for Changing

Now that we've worked hard to create the best possible ground for our group members to develop awarenesses and take risks, it is important to remain vigilant. A metaphor which appeals to me is gardening. Ruth Ronall and I had a lot of fun once comparing a group to a garden in an article entitled "The Gestalt Therapy Group as Fertile Ground for Growth" [unpublished; available on request].

If you are a serious gardener like I am, you probably recall the excitement of the fore-contact: perusing catalogs, ordering seeds and plants, deciding which plants will work well with each other, and sketching the plot. Then comes the early direct contact: turning over the soil, spading in friable additives such as sawdust. This is followed by the 'first session' – the seeding and planting. After this intriguing 'session', there it is and it begins to grow. Yet as any gardener knows, there is a lot yet to be done to maintain this promising project: mulching, watering, weeding, staking, tying, midseason fertilizing, pinching, deadheading, etc. If you are not a gardener, some of these terms may not mean much, yet I'm sure you get the picture.

And so it is with the group. I [or we if there are co-therapists] have diligently and excitedly created it. Let's say the first session went well and also the next few. Soon the infatuation stage has passed and it is now the steady ongoing so-called middle phase. I read once that of therapy's three phases, the beginning and the ending have built-in excitement and intrigue. Yet no less important is the plodding middle phase. And part of the work in the middle phase is to maintain the ground that's been created. Let's see if I can apply my gardening metaphors:

*mulching: mulch is to hold in moisture, inhibit weeds and provide nutrients. Applied to the group would be introducing creative events, such as using music or poetry or movement [see Ch 14], varying the format, self-revelation, occasional parties or celebrations of client achievements, etc. All these 'moisten' and 'provide nutrients. 'Inhibiting weeds' would include moving the pace along and discouraging bullshitting and storytelling [unless the latter serves a therapeutic purpose].

*watering and fertilizing: the group needs these vital ingredients just as plants do. Being very alert, attentive, creative, empathic and authentic are ways the therapist can nourish the group. Members can contribute too and letting them know they have some responsibility for the vitality of the group often brings out the gardener in them too. Additionally, occasionally I give a mini-lecture at propitious moments, sometimes along the lines of my model for changing and other times on anything I think can be useful to the membership. Also I occasionally give a handout to perk things up [e.g., see Appendix A: "Embrace/Avoid"].

*weeding: in addition to the above, on rare occasions I will suggest to a member, after exhausting other attempts and as a last resort, that he leave the group because of extreme toxicity or group disruptiveness. I have only done this twice in 45 years.

*pinching: pinching is something experienced gardeners do with certain plants to promote maximum flower size. If a dahlia stem, for instance, has 2 or 3 flower buds, removing all but one will maximize the size of the remaining bud. If a group is all over the place, jumping from one issue to another without enough time being spent on each, I will urge staying with one now and leaving the others for later. Similarly if a member is being interrupted at a crucial point, even if with goodwill, I will exercise my authority and ask the interrupter to back off and let me guide the work. I will also be active to limit advice-giving. That's what I'm paid for after all.

*staking, tying and deadheading: these are all ways to support the plant's growth. So, transferring to group, keep in mind that one must pay attention to how the group is progressing, and if it is not progressing as well as you think it can, then do something. That can mean being more active or possibly being less active; or more suggestive of experiments or exploring what is happening that is bottling the group up, etc.

Applying these principles to our sample session, note that a number of my interventions had the goal, and hopefully the effect, of injecting some novelty and creativity into the session: asking Donna to imagine a melody, suggesting Camilla place her hand on her heart and listen to what it had to say. Other interventions designed, among other purposes, to maintain the ground include self-revelation, being consistent with the ending time, challenging Jason to take responsibility for the vitality of the group, bringing Donna back to the present when she began storytelling, including all members through rounds. Although not illustrated in this particular session, another effort in this direction in subsequent sessions included ultimately refusing to let Jack rejoin the group after he was unmanageable and quit and then wanted to return; Also turning the group over to Donna for one whole session when she put on a wonderfully creative show depicting her life. At other times I brought some goodies into the session as did others.

I will leave the reader, if so inclined, to assign the metaphors [mulching, pinching, etc] to these interventions.

Chapter 10. Experimenting/Risking

Gestalt therapy is deservedly famous for its emphasis on experimenting – and groups provide an exceptionally good medium for this.

Exercises and Experiments

First I want to distinguish between 'exercises' and experiments or risks, as I view them. Both are useful, though only experiments and other risks lead directly to interpersonal changing. An exercise is an activity with a designed purpose, usually suggested by the leader, frequently without a risk. An experiment is an activity designed to discover something and often has a risk attached to it.

An example of an exercise is "Let's all close our eyes and pay attention to our bodies" or "Imagine what your life would be like in five years if it were to be perfect". The first of these may be designed to enhance awareness in the moment &/or to increase members' ability to tune into their bodies. The second may have the purpose of providing direction to the work. I say 'may' in both cases since the exact purposes would depend on the context.

Here is an example of an experiment with regard to a particular member named Sally who is weak on self-assertion. Let's say she has just been ordered to keep quiet by Alan, another member. Sally trembles, her jaws tighten, yet says nothing. After these obvious physical changes are pointed out and she is suggested to notice what she experiences in her body, she is asked to silently imagine what she would like to say to Alan. When she acknowledges getting in touch with this, she is offered the option of saying this directly to Alan. Perhaps she can ...and does with obvious discomfort. Or perhaps she cannot and is then offered the suggestion to whisper to her best friend in the group what she would like to say out loud. Perhaps she is able to do this, though tentatively. Or perhaps she cannot do even this. In all of these cases, she has discovered something. In the first instance she has discovers that she can voice her objection. She may also discover some unpleasant consequences [which of course are unknown in advance]. In the second she has discovered that she can imagine it yet not say it directly. In the third she has discovered she cannot even whisper it to a friend. This has been an experiment...because the behavior is perceived as risky and unfamiliar by Sally and has grown organically out of the events in the group. There is no fixed agenda or purpose other than to explore an alternative to her fixed pattern and to see what she discovers. Of course, this is not the end of the matter. In the first instance Alan will probably have some reaction. In the second, perhaps I might ask "So how does this feel?"and if I think it wise I might wonder if she can now say it to Alan. In the third I might ask, "So what is your objection to whispering this to your friend?" Or any number of possible interventions...and so far we haven't considered what all the others in the group might express or do.

The Essential ground

From my point of view, all my efforts and all the preceding events leading up to and surrounding this experiment constitute the foundation on which the experiments and risks rests, or more accurately the foundation on which Sally stands, enabling her to accept them. More specifically I mean each and every aspect already discussed: the initial preparation and literature, the selection of members, the initial session, the relationship between Sally and me, etc. (All the mulching, watering etc.) Nothing matters unless the experiments and risks take place and they can only take place if the ground supports them. The more supported and safer the members feel, the more he is willing to risk. This is why we, at least I, build the group and develop group cohesion and self-reveal and promote democratic process – to develop and provide the ground for experiments and other risks.

Another way of saying this is that the group is of little or no value without risking and experimenting. Awareness is good and feeling connected to others is fine, yet they are mainly valuable as preparation for experimenting or risking, the essentials for changing. I think it is fair to say that gestalt therapy was created in response to the realization that psychoanalysis often brought insight....yet not changing. Although Fritz Perls at times said all that is required is awareness, I disagree [and he probably disagreed with this too, at least in some of his utterances]. After awareness, clients are able to dissolve fixed gestalten, or patterns, only by experimenting with new ones. It is not enough to be aware of the old pattern and how it evolved. Actively sweating out alternatives is essential. And the group is a great arena for that.

This is by no means a novel discovery by me. There are many examples of this in the literature. One appealing little book which recently came to my attention is *How People Change* by Alan Wheelis [1975]. He says, for instance "Personality change follows change in behavior. Since we are what we do, if we want to change what we are we must begin by changing what we do, *must undertake a new mode of action* [italics mine p. 101].

Repetition

Of course it isn't that easy. One experiment or risk shines a light on what is possible in living. Yet unless this new capability is built on through attentive repetition, the new behavior will fade and the old pattern remains unchanged. This was a conundrum to me for a long time. If a person was capable of doing it once, say self-asserting, why didn't the person just do it all the time from here on out, rather than reverting to submissiveness. One day some animal research came to my attention and gave me a plausible explanation. In this research it was found that old established patterns are resistant to extinction and that about eighteen months of behaving differently are necessary before the old neural tracts fade out and new ones dominate...at least in hamsters.

So I tell my clients "You need to repeat this as often as you can – in group, and in life -- for a long time, maybe eighteen months, before your new way is firmly established ". And even then, in line with the previous quote from Angyal [1965, p. 260] under great stress the old pattern may re-emerge...yet I think, and Angyal thinks, it is easier to reestablish the new this time, as the stress is overcome or recedes. Because I value repetition so much, one item on my Group Therapy Log [Appendix A] asks "If you experimented with doing something novel tonight, how can you practice it in your daily life? Be as specific as possible".

Reluctance, Fear and Terror

Risky experiments obviously bring up levels of fear in group members. Speaking a little loosely, I characterize these levels as reluctance, fear and terror – in other words trepidation in ascending degrees.

On the mildest level, a member will demur from the experiment by saying something like "I can't do that" or "I'm too embarrassed to do that" or "That's too silly", etc. On the next level, the member will own to being scared, afraid, or fearful – all pretty much the same. On the most intense level members will experience and may articulate being terrified to enter into the experiment.

In all cases I strongly urge the therapist to refrain from any kind of arm-twisting or pressuring. I do believe it is okay and useful to instead follow the client's lead with such questions as "Okay, it is strictly your decision. Yet are you willing to tell us what you experience when you hear me suggest this experiment?" or "What's going on in your body? And in your head?" Or "Okay, yet are you willing to tell us what your objection is?"

Sometimes this may lead to a working through of the fear and then a willingness to experiment. A lot depends how desperate the person is....the more desperate the more willing to leap.

Our Sample Session

In a sense my suggesting to Walt that we explore his mistrust of me was asking him to risk. He demurred and I had no leverage, so let it go. Later when Kim noted that in four years she had yet to do a round, I didn't push her, believing just saying that was a lot for her. With Camilla, though, I judged her to be ready to try a round. She was flustered and anxious, yet with some gentle support was able to risk this.

Chapter 11.
More about the Therapist

As has been well-established by research, and consistent with common sense, the person of the therapist is the single most important factor in the therapeutic equation, more important that the particular 'school' of treatment. In gestalt therapy there has been an evolution of therapeutic style over time.

The Fritz Perls Model

Whether he meant his style to be imitated or not, Fritz Perls had a great influence in shaping the attitude of early gestalt group therapists. My shorthand characterization of his attitude is "irresponsible". By this I mean an approach that placed insufficient emphasis on the therapist's responsibility to maximize the likelihood that the therapeutic contact would be beneficial to the client. Much of this influence was conveyed through the films that were made of Fritz working in groups using his hot seat method. Although at times he was patient and supportive, at others he was impatient and irascible, leaning on his famous dictum "I'll do my thing and you do yours" as well as the aforementioned "Wipe your own ass". My observation is that he was much more patient and supportive of women than of men. In any case, he did not evince a dedicated effort to create and maintain the group atmosphere that I've spoken about. This is not overly surprising since he was mainly doing demonstrations not ongoing therapy. Unfortunately others extrapolated from the one format [demonstrations] to the other [ongoing treatment], bringing into the latter too much of this cavalier attitude. One particularly destructive way this seeped into group work was the notion that is was okay to sleep with a group member. As we know now [and probably knew then] this is often a formula for disaster.

Responsibility

The above attitude prevailed until roughly 1980 when a next generation began to voice concerns [Feder, 1980; Melnick et al, 1994]. This was augmented by the waning of the hippie culture and a drift back to more responsible values. By 1990 or so, gestalt therapy had in this sense joined the mainstream, maturing into a fully responsible therapeutic approach. In other ways gestalt therapy has remained somewhat outside the mainstream – referring to its holistic, contactful and experimental emphases, as well as its generally liberal attitudes politically and culturally. For example, gestalt therapy embraced homosexuality as equal to heterosexuality long before the rest of the therapeutic community.

What I mean by responsibility is that ideally everything the therapist does should be geared toward the welfare of the client. This means all interventions be based on judicious and reasonable intentions. Obviously therapists are human and will make mistakes, both of out of poor or incorrect judgment as well as out of personal limitations and weaknesses. Despite all the personal therapy and supervision possible, human frailty will still prevail at times. The idea is for these errors to be minimal, and whenever possible to be owned and turned into therapeutic benefit.

The Human Element

Two recent studies [Bedi, 2005; Lilliengren, 2005] give us other information besides the somewhat dry comments just made regarding responsibility. These two studies, done in tandem, concern the creation of the therapeutic alliance. Very interestingly, clients enumerated the following events or incidents or behaviors as critical in promoting what the authors call the 'curative' factor -

*nonverbal expressions of interest, like eye contact and leaning forward

*remembering what was said in an earlier session; paraphrasing

*self-disclosure, especially along lines of "Yes, I've been there, too"

*encouraging comments

*greetings and farewells, including hugging, smiling

*openness to criticisms

*offering tissues when client cries

*offering food and drink

*meeting after hours in very stressful times or emergencies

*giving a home phone number

*humor and laughter

One common thread running through these factors is something so central to gestalt therapy, namely 'good' contact. A major goal in gestalt therapy is to promote the ability of clients to make good contact. And a major contributor to reaching this, and other, goals is making good contact ourselves with clients. This applies equally to group therapy as to other forms. One difference, of course, is that group therapy involves contacting a number of people at the same time. Some therapists may not find this as comfortable or compatible with their own natures as making good contact with one person at a time. This each therapist has to discover for himself. As mentioned in my introduction to this booklet I have enjoyed groups early on...and you?

I am not advocating any particular way of being as a person in the group other than to be as authentic as possible *within the role.* Of paramount concern is the welfare of the members; at times this will speak against complete authenticity. Suppose, for instance, a particular member turns me on sexually. This might appropriately be mentioned at some relevant point, yet nurturing and making a show of this reaction in most cases would probably be detrimental to the group's development. The idea is to have the feeling, own it in a relevant exchange and compartmentalize it. The exception might be in a very experienced, cohesive mature group capable of handling this. Similarly with favorites. From what I've heard, most therapists have favorite clients; I know I do. And though I may unavoidably be subtly warmer to them, it is incumbent on me to keep the wraps on these feelings and provide each client with as much nourishing support as possible. A lot of vigilance is required here.

Dual Relationships

The studies mentioned above by Bedi and Lilliengren were particularly pleasing to me because of my own take on what is fitting within gestalt therapy. In 2004 an article by me was published by the *Gestalt Review* entitled *"Dual Relationships: A Gestalt Therapy Perspective"*. I received a lot of appreciation for the article – also a lot of flak. 'Dual relationships' is the term used when a therapist has, in addition to the therapeutic contact, an interaction with a client of a personal, social or business nature. It is also named boundary-crossing by some. Examples are: playing tennis with a client [personal], attending a client's wedding [social], buying a car from, or selling tennis tickets to, a client [business]. In my article I argue that as an experimental and experiential approach, gestalt therapy can be friendly towards such interactions, provided that they are engaged in thoughtfully, judiciously and responsibly, and with the clients' welfare still foremost. As an example of such a social activity, it has been my custom each year during the winter holiday season to have a festive dinner at a restaurant with my weekly group in lieu of a final session of the year, provided the group wants to do this. And at these social events, I have allowed the group to treat me to dinner if they so chose, which I guess borders on a business transaction. And I have on occasions had open house for clients at my home during the holiday season. Groups in particular lend themselves to such events, particularly marathon groups [see Ch. 12], and more so when they are residential. In these we not only work together but live together and have much interaction of a personal and social nature and financial nature [splitting costs for food, for instance]. Again the therapist must feel comfortable with this type of contact with his clients, and I believe, if he does, the ground for experimenting and risking in sessions is strengthened

More about self-disclosure

There are many ways to self-disclose in a group. Of course the interest in and tolerance for doing so varies greatly from therapist to therapist. For instance, one's office can reveal a good deal about the practitioner. In my case I have moved my office often and sometimes practiced from my home. My next to last office required clients to walk past my kitchen, my bathroom and dining room, through my living room and into the consulting room. I have heard many therapists say that they would never have such a set-up. Why not? What's to hide? We all eat; we all shit; we all have certain styles we prefer, mine being quite casual and old-fashioned mostly. I love plants and whenever possible have them hanging in windows. So by the time a new client reaches the consulting room, if she's not too anxious to observe she already knows a good deal about me. True, an occasional client is turned off – it's not professional enough.

In the group, many opportunities for self-revelation and transparency arise, more so than in individual therapy. More people are noticing you and picking up on your mood, your health, your idiosyncrasies – and some may comment on what they notice. So if a client in a group comments that I look tired, if I am I will say so [and of course this can be grist for the mill]. Illness, especially serious illness, poses a particular challenge. I know of one therapist, who generally I thought was excellent, become incapacitated yet refuse to acknowledge the severity of the illness, leading to a rupture in the relationship. She repeatedly cancelled sessions and wouldn't discuss it. At the extreme I once had a client come to me specifically for focalized counseling around her therapist's death. Although perceptibly very sick, he denied it – until one day she arrived at his office to find a sign on the door "Dr X has died". What can be more existential than death! If we value that our approach is existential, this has clear implications, one of which is that we are all humans in this perplexing journey together. As Laura Perls put it: "One of our main goals is to help our clients live with *uncertainty without anxiety*" [1992, p.155].

In groups we often do rounds. If I suggest a round, I may participate in it, especially if it is a tough one. If a moment in the work comes up, for instance, at which I suggest the following round: "Consider saying something to us that you are ashamed of" I will include myself in this experience – and deal with any fallout.

Now there is a big difference between useful self-disclosing and self-disclosing which hinders the process. What is useful is being an active participant in the organic flow of the group.

What hinders is spurious information about yourself. I have often been told by new clients that one thing they didn't like about a previous therapist is that he rambled on about his family or his achievements, etc. Being an authentic participant is conducive to cohesiveness and supportiveness in the group, part of the essential ground for risking. Of course at times this means tarnishing your image, which of course is painful. In the long run, though, it is more helpful than harmful. Recently a graduate student consulted me [informally, by email] about her intense anxiety about a forthcoming demonstration of group therapy she was required to do with her supervisor present.

She wondered how she should start the session, so as to minimize the others being aware of her nervousness. I advised her to do the opposite, to tell everyone exactly what she was feeling and thinking and fearing. She had the guts to do so, and the results were excellent. It is not shameful to be nervous or worried. It is human. My own therapist, many years ago, during one session was drenched with perspiration. "Al" I said "I can't help but notice that you're sweating a lot. Are you okay?" He told me that he was very worried about his wife due to an illness. I offered, as an experienced therapist myself, to help him with his worries. He declined. As a result, though, of this openness, he was again able to focus on me. And other human touches by him helped me feel affection for him and to trust him [I was in deep shit at the time, very depressed – actually here I am self-disclosing to you. How does that impact you?].

Co-therapists

It is fairly common for therapists to work together in groups. This has both advantages and challenges. Taking the advantages first it provides:

*more than one parental or authority figure for clients to connect with in a nourishing way; also to get in trouble with [that is to connect with in accordance with one or more of their troublesome *fixed gestalten*]

*support for one another, i.e. for the two therapists
*opportunities to discuss plans, strategies, problems, creative ideas, etc

*different ways of looking at situations, thus more options

*the benefits of synergy, ideally

There are problematic possibilities too, when:

*the chemistry between the two is or becomes poor

*when the styles don't mesh, which can deaden the process [though not necessarily damage the relationship between the two.

The situation is a little different with trainees. It is hierarchical, in that I make it clear at the outset that this is *my* group, these are *my* clients so I have the last word. Of course I welcome suggestions and active input, and enjoyed processing afterwards, though again the hierarchy is clear.

In marathons for the most part I have worked with my closest friends, loving friends. These have been great experiences with great chemistry and excellent results. I have had two unsatisfactory experiences, though, with therapists with whom I wasn't especially close. We didn't mesh. In one case, in private practice,

I made the mistake of agreeing to do a weekend marathon with a woman I didn't much like and whom I had seen be very malicious and rigid. About a quarter of the way through the weekend, she accused me of trying to upstage her and to destroy her relationships with her clients, whom she had enlisted into the marathon. I found no way to appease her and the creative adjustment we made was that for the rest of the weekend I would work with my clients in one room and she with hers in another.

We never spoke again after that weekend. In another instance, at a conference I agreed to work with a woman I liked but whose style I wasn't very familiar with. It turned out she was much more structured and formal than I. I never felt comfortable and though we did some good work, I never felt unleashed or very creative. It didn't damage our relationship yet I wouldn't want to work with her again.

This all reminds me of playing doubles in tennis. I enjoy it much more and feel freer and more creative when playing with someone I have a good emotional connection with. The moral of the story is to choose carefully. It may not always work out and yet some forethought might avoid unsatisfying outcomes.

Training and Preparation

I suggest the following to enable a gestalt therapist – that is one well grounded and experienced in individual work - to become an equally skilled gestalt group therapist:

*several years of participation in a gestalt therapy group as a member;

*several years of participation in a gestalt therapy group as an assistant to an experienced gestalt group therapist, who would of course provide guidance, mentoring and supervision;

*several years in an experiential/didactic gestalt group therapy training group or program, one which provides ample opportunity to process the work, that is to review it with an eye on both gestalt therapy principles and group dynamic principles, as illustrated in the experiential component;

*a grounding in relevant readings, again concerning both gestalt group therapy and group dynamics; many training programs include such readings – and discussions of them – in the training experience;

*then about five years of running a group – now you think you've got it. Fortunately learning never ends, which means there's little chance of boredom in a group, as new challenges and new insights emerge. So it's a good idea to be in a peer supervision group – forever [it's usually fun and nourishing too].

Styles and Outcomes

This paragraph is purely a speculative one, something I have longed wanted to research [or more accurately hoped that someone else would research]. I refer to the relationship between personal therapeutic styles and members' outcomes. For example, my hunch is that challenging in-your-face therapists elicit outcomes characterized by members become more assertive and self-supportive while gentler more cautious therapists elicit outcomes characterized by growth in compassion and

120

tolerance for others' neurotic tendencies. Perhaps this will stimulate some Ph. D. student to candidate to come with a research design on these hypotheses for her doctoral dissertation. Long ago Kurt Lewin and associates [1939] famously studied the effects of three different leaderships styles [autocratic, democratic and laissez-faire] on working groups. Similar work with reference to the effects of leadership characteristics on therapy groups might also prove useful.

Summary

The therapist is key to the group's usefulness. The more authentic, *contactful*, consistent, fair, warm, etc the therapist is, the better it is for the group. This is all in addition to 'knowledgability', training and experience which of course are also major contributors. With regard to co-therapists, it's like parenting. The better the relationship between the parents [therapists] and the more in harmony they are in practices, the more conducive is this to a nourishing effective family [group]. And, as I indicated, I speculate that different styles evoke different outcomes.

Chapter 12. Other Kinds of Groups

In addition to therapy groups, there are quite a few related groups which bear mentioning. Here is a little about each.

Marathon Groups

This term, perhaps not as popular as it once was, refers to groups of an extended length, rather than your weekly 90-minute or 2-hour group. It could be an all-day session, a weekend or even a week. It is useful to have co-leaders because of the taxing nature of such groups, though often leaders go it solo. Generally there are more participants than in a weekly group, usually from 10-20. One exception to this in my experience is when an ongoing weekly group has an all-day or weekend experience. In this case, only members of the ongoing group are present and the number is thus smaller, in my case 8.

Marathon groups have the advantages of allowing not only longer work with an individual but also more intensive work. Marathons allow the leader to pursue extremely fragmenting work. On several occasions I have been part of a therapeutic team in a marathon where the protagonist of the moment had a psychotic break. This can be very scary to all present, including the therapists, yet the time frame permits this to be played out with ample opportunity for recovery and great benefit to the participant in question. She can go to her most feared place and come back.

Ordinarily in marathons there is a wide variety of work: hot seat, interactive, creative artwork, etc. And marathons, especially residentials, are noteworthy for the boundary-crossing which is almost inevitable. Members and leaders share the same space: shop together, eat together, share chores, play together, etc. This creates a very human bond which provides an excellent ground for the work.

One special problem which sometimes crops up in marathons concerns the histories with one another which the participants may have. An example of this is a marathon I did in England. I knew none of the participants in advance or their intertwined histories. It soon came out that two of the women hated each other. One was the ex-wife of a participant and another his present wife – the present wife had 'stolen' him form the first wife. So the first order of business was to deal with this. Before long they were wrestling animatedly and hostilely in the middle of the floor, screaming at each other. Ordinarily I don't allow physical fighting; somehow I intuited it would be okay this time. No one won the wrestling match, in fact they ended up laughing. During the rest of the weekend they spent a lot of time talking things out and by the end of the marathon they were great pals. One moral of this story is, if you don't know the participants' histories, ask in an early round "Who knows whom and how does it feel to be in this group with him or her?" You might be surprised.

For some good chapters on marathons see Mintz, 1980 and Aylward, 1996.

Supervision &/or Training Groups

Some people consider these groups separately. My own approach is to combine these functions into one group. To be a little clearer, in a supervision group members bring in cases they are working with, often when they are stuck or experiencing problems. In a training group, the focus is on teaching, both didactically and/or experientially, and may not include case supervision.

As I said my approach, at least in recent years, has been to offer an ongoing group experience with opportunity for both. There are many ways to go about this in terms of schedule and membership. What I have preferred is a group that meets monthly for a full day for eight or nine months. If we can work it out sometimes we end with a weekend residential. I also, a la the NY Institute informal approach, accept members at all levels of experience. The way I work it, if there are openings [many people return year after year] new people can try the group out for one session. After the second session no one may enter the group until next year.

The content and activities of these meetings of mine are determined by the group. Sometimes a session starts off with an hour or so of an interactive group; we do case supervision, discuss agreed-upon readings or topics; have opportunity for in vivo supervision as members work with one another. Etc. I like this "Okay, what shall we do this year [month]?" approach. On the other hand many [probably most] institutes and trainers have set curricula, sometimes for up to four years with the same group together for the whole time.

Most training/supervision groups differ from normal therapy groups. The primary focus is on learning, the secondary focus is on personal growth. I said 'most' however because some trainers/supervisors teach primarily via the experiential method; that is, the members learn by their own experience in the group, which is run as a therapy group, with little didactic effort by the leader. Laura Perls followed this model and a few people still do. Personally, I like to be very clear that time is reserved for processing, thinking, discussing and even for a mini-lecture here and there. I also encourage members to bring in any special skills they have and lead us in their particular ways. So sometimes we have a member leading using writing, movement, dance, bodywork, etc.

Peer Groups

Many gestalt group therapists are members of peer groups, also called peer supervision groups or inter-vision groups. I was part of one or another for over twenty years and it was a very important part of my professional life with strong personal overtones. In addition to case supervision, we also did personal work and we often arranged for playtime. One time that stands out is a day we spent together on Fire Island. As a result we became very close and trusting – with the occasional conflict. I recommend this highly and it's not necessary, in my opinion, to wait until one has finished training to join such a group. Obviously there is no evaluative function and no leader, so there is more freedom to expose one's vulnerabilities and to be as creative as desired. Perhaps some institutes 'forbid' them; if so, I'm not aware of it.

Homogeneous/Theme Groups

There are numerous varieties of groups: men's, women's, people with aids, addictions, etc. Basically the principles enumerated in the previous chapters all apply, the main difference being in the more narrow selection process. For an example of such a group see Perry Klepner's case study of a group whose members all have the HIV [1996]. And then there have been some brave souls who have applied this group work to persons who carry the diagnosis 'borderline personality disorder'...not just one, possibly two, such persons in one group, but a group consisting *entirely* of such individuals. See Schoenberg [1999]. A more common approach, and much more tolerable, is to place one such person, relatively high functioning in the diagnostic category, in a heterogeneous group [Greenberg, E. and Hahn, A., 2001]

Chapter 13. Odds and Ends

In this chapter I will include a number of pieces which haven't yet been touched on or which need some elaboration.

Rituals

It is useful during the life of a group to enact some organically relevant, meaningful and acceptable rituals. For instance in the sample session, if Walt's departure had been a typical one – in which he gave us a month's notice – we could have marked his last session with some form of ritual. Many possibilities come to mind:

devoting the last half hour to some edibles and some appreciation of his contributions; some singing; a gift for him, etc. Other rituals for other occasions might revolve around milestones in members' lives, including the therapist's; or achievements in the outer world, etc. Ideally these should be on target and succinct, taking enough time to make an impact and not so much as to dilute the process. Usually I prefer them toward the end of the session and of course with the group's permission and approval, and often its initiative.

Contacts outside of group

There are several points of view regarding members having contact with one another outside of group:

*forbid it

*take no position

*tell them it's up to them yet ask for agreement that anything of significance between or among group members outside of group be considered "grist for the mill" during group; a corollary of this is that it is 'illegal' to press another member to keep secret any event outside of group between two members.

My own position is the last and I make it explicit in information I give clients [see the 'Group Therapy Agreement' in Appendix A]. Two experiences have led me to this, one as a group member, the other as a group leader.

As a member of an analytic group before I discovered gestalt therapy, we were enjoined by the analyst/group leader from having any contact with one another outside of group. This rule was widely broken, without discussion in group, diluting the power of the group in my view.

And as a leader, a very sticky event occurred outside of group between a single female member and a married male member. They had a friendship which led to sex. Just before culminating the sex act, he swore her to secrecy from the group. She was also in individual therapy with me and told me about it. I encouraged her to bring it up in group, since that was our agreement. When she finally did, there was a lot of relief, among other feelings, in the group. The group had bogged down for some weeks and after this came to life again. I am convinced this secret was the sand in the motor.

Beyond this, I view gestalt therapy as focusing on contact and openness and forbidding natural contact is inconsistent with gestalt therapy principles. As I write this I remember that I made two very close friends stemming from our being members of the same group. Of course, this was in the early '70's when boundary crossing was almost synonymous with gestalt Therapy, so it wasn't an issue. It is important, though, that significant interactions outside of group be brought into group and explored, and be treated just as any other interaction between or among members.

Departures and Arrivals

Although I've touched on this before, I want to say a little more. The essential point is that anytime a new person enters a group or an old person leaves a group, it is in now a *new* group. Granted, like earthquakes, the seismic reading can be anywhere from very small up to very great, yet it is a mistake to just go on as if nothing worth attending to has happened. Always attend to this to the degree appropriate to the impact. This could be ten minutes...or ten sessions.

When a new person enters, according to my longest group client [17 years], it takes two months for the group to get back to where it was in terms of trust and depth. Of course, this is just an opinion yet as a rule of thumb, I think it's pretty sharp. The implication here is don't push the group too hard right after a new person has arrived. Let the group find its way back to where it was. Do this by being a little laid back, making some observations or inquiries centering around the new person – not pushing him as much as acknowledging his presence, as well as exploring the group members' feelings about this development.

When there is a departure, different members [and the leader] will likely have different reactions. Some may be relieved, some may be sad, some may be angry, etc. Explore them fully and allow time for them to be integrated before moving on to other business.

Shame

The experience of shame in a therapy group is heightened by the presence of multiple others. Naturally. So the therapist must be very cautious in this regard. One experience of shame can be sufficient to cause a member to leave abruptly and permanently. I have made some mistakes as a leader which have led to this. On one occasion

I joked about a member's stiffness. Trying to be funny, I was lethal. So I've learned.

Recently an obese client [over 300 pounds] told me in individual session that he was very troubled by his overweight and that he would like to bring it up in group and find out how his obesity impacted on the others. He said he didn't know if he would have the courage to initiate it. He asked me if I would bring it up. I agreed to do so if I saw he couldn't. About halfway through the next session, when it was apparent he as unable to, I brought it up, telling the group that Mark and I had made this arrangement. So I led the discussion, being very careful to provide enough protection for Mark so that he could tolerate this very painful encounter. And after about a half-hour I moved the focus from Mark and asked other members to talk about their insecurities over aspects of their physical beings. Without this help, Mark wouldn't have been able to begin work on this very important piece, so in my view it was perfectly fine for me to help him get into it and to deflect from him when I sensed he had reached a saturation point. Without such assistance and guidance he might have been either too ashamed to start it or too hurt to continue. So be careful, since leaders' biases and predispositions about certain types of people can leak out and cause damage.

Violation of ground Rules

Every group has rules as well of course as norms [see next paragraph]. A rule is something that has been directly articulated, either by the leader alone or by the group democratically. In most cases I have found it better to bring up violations as grist for the mill, rather than have any penalties or specific consequences. For instance suppose a group has a rule that all energy must be directed at group events, not outside events, and a member continually violates that by bringing up his job [something like this often occurs]. As leader, after frequent requests to no avail, I will then say let's look at this and explore what this does for you, what are you getting out of it. Invariably I find that a frequently violated rule has a lot of meaning and purpose and obviously it is counterproductive, probably with parallels in the person's life. So exploring it can be quite significant and beneficial – much more than any kind of penalty.

I have made a few exceptions in instances of excessive disruption, including frequent walking out of sessions. At some point, after failing to accomplish anything by working on it, I will draw a line and stick to it. For example I did tell a member who had become very fragile and paranoid that if he stormed out midsession one more time I would consider the group inappropriate for him and ask him to drop out. He did it again and I followed through on my warning [obviously the group was too much for him and …well, it's a long sad story].

Group norms

Norms usually evolve over time, often subtly and with minimal awareness. For example, a group may have a rule or an agreement to start at 8 pm, yet over time members come a little late and the group doesn't get 'started' until 8:15 [actually it has started at 8, the start being characterized as avoidant]. This will continue until someone highlights it: it could be a member who is very angry about it or feels hurt by it [which bear exploring] or by the leader, whatever he feels, including guilty for letting it happen. Other common norms are: a great deal

138

of deflective humor; avoidance of certain topics, such as sexual attraction within the group; ignoring silent members etc.

Group shrinkage

As I mentioned before, groups were much more popular 30 years ago and it was much easier to maintain optimal group size: if someone left, someone was waiting in the wings to replace her. This is no longer my experience and many therapists have told me it is no longer true for them either. As a result it may be necessary to have smaller groups at least for a time, groups of five or even four. This isn't good -- yet it is not a catastrophe either. One modification is to shorten the group; another is to meet less often, say three times a month instead of four; also when this occurred in my interactive group, I relaxed the rule and allowed for wider-ranging work.

Of course the idea is to rebuild the group as soon as possible. Hopefully this is a phase and if and when the culture loosens up again, group may become more popular.

Individual and Group Therapy Combined

Often one or more members of an ongoing weekly group will also be in individual therapy, either with the group therapist or another therapist. If it is with another therapist some communication between the two therapists is a good idea [with a release of course]. This can be useful if the client enters a crisis phase so that the two work in a consistent manner. Also if the group therapist is working in any kind of unusual way, it's a good idea that the individual therapist knows something about it and hopefully can support it.

If the group therapist is also providing a group member with individual therapy there are some pitfalls to avoid. Some therapists minimize that by having a policy of not discussing the group during individual. I prefer to eschew this policy. Instead I let the client know that I will not discuss any other member of the group during individual time – any issue the client has with that person needs to be taken back to the group. I won't necessarily try to stifle the client in individual from talking about the group, though I don't encourage it. If the client does bring up an issue concerning the group I try to support the client to bring his issue back into the group and to focus the client on how he can use the group productively.

As mentioned above with reference to the obese client Mark, sometimes during individual I make a deal with a client regarding supporting him in certain situations. Usually, most of the clients in my groups have either been in individual with me in the past or are in the present; some, however, are referred for group by their individual therapists.

Couples in a Group

Occasionally I have had a couple in the same group. I think its more trouble than it's worth and don't recommend it. Yet sometimes a couple emerges from meeting in a group, so there they are. My policy is not to ask either or both to leave, but to ask them to avoid doing couples work in the group. If they need it [most couples do] then get some couples therapy. Certainly they can address each other in the group or have an issue that is right there in the group – but spare us conflicts over who does more housework or wastes money on trifles, etc.

Confluence

To some gestalt folk confluence is a dirty word, suggesting avoidance of conflict or differentiation. Certainly that can be true. Yet there is also healthy confluence, a short-lived period when the group is in total harmony. This usually results from some intense experience during which all personal issues fade for a while. One example in my experience was on Sept 11, 2001. Living only twelve miles from the World Trade Center, seeing the smoke all day in reality as well as on TV, knowing persons in the buildings, nothing else was of importance that evening when the group met as scheduled. We were as one with our shock, our worry, our fears. On the other hand, when a group is harmonious and/or bland for an extended period this needs to be addressed. The therapist needs to be very active in exploring what is being hidden and what that is all about.

Chapter 14. Beyond Talk

Laura Perls was wont to say that there are as many gestalt therapies as there are gestalt therapists, meaning each therapist has strengths which she can bring into play. In her case, she worked a great deal with movement, more than many.

I think one can also say there are as many gestalt therapies as there are gestalt clients, meaning clients have specialties too which can be brought into the work.

This is as true of group work as it is on individual work. So it is very useful for the therapist to be aware of her client's particular interests and skills. I mentioned in our sample session, for instance, that Donna had a talent for performing, so I welcomed her bringing it into the group one night and both entertaining us and also expressing herself at a very deep level. Other clients have brought their poetry, their music, their baking, their dance, their yoga, their meditation, their massage skills, etc., all in addition to their feedback and their ideas for experiments.

One of the beauties of gestalt therapy is our openness to all aspects of expression. Many therapies limit themselves to talk. This is unnatural. The human being is multifaceted and so should therapy be. So as a group therapist be aware of your own and your clients' interests and talents and incorporate them into the sessions. This said, I want to stress that it is best to do so appropriately, judiciously and organically.

Marathons in particular with their luxury of time – and sometimes of place, as in the example following *lend themselves particularly to this expansion of the work.

One example that I recall vividly is described in the previously mentioned chapter by my co-therapist Jack Aylward [1996, p. 249]. In this incident an overly self-controlled fellow ends his piece of work by standing on the back deck overlooking the Atlantic Ocean and throws

144

objects [tennis balls, grapefruit – whatever is at hand and which the group scrums up for him] into the sea. This arose organically out of the work [I recommend reading the chapter] and out of Norman's experience as a baseball player and his love of the game. Here he is bringing this interest and skill into a deeper level of expression.

Obviously such an activity isn't always available – fortuitously we had rented a house on the beach for that weekend. Yet in any group diligent attention to such possibilities often leads to unexpected emerging creative moments. They might be group exercises, again arising out of the content and out of the particular interests and skills of those particular members – and in context of where this particular group is at this moment. I would not ordinarily, for instance, suggest anything intimate in the first sessions – such as massage or tender touch or dancing together, whereas this might be perfectly correct and useful after the group has reached a stage of much greater closeness. Gauge the suggestion to the stage and mood of the group.

Chapter 15.
Community and Educational Applications

Strictly speaking, this chapter and the next are extrapolations from the topic of group therapy, yet I think they are related closely enough to be mentioned, albeit briefly.

Community Applications

I have found that my training and experience as a group therapist have served me well in my community endeavors, which usually involve groups. I refer to a variety of my involvements: political [such as the Green party], sporting [my tennis club], professional [the local Mental Health Association], etc. I am sure most people can relate to these connections from their own particular affiliations. We trained group therapists can bring to these groups our skills and perspectives which the average person cannot do. For example, I recently attended a meeting of the Outreach Committee of the Berkeley Progressive Alliance. It took place in somebody's living room and I was a complete newcomer. The others all knew each other. I watched as they wrestled with their task of coming up with a plank for the alliance's platform for the upcoming municipal elections. I didn't say much, just listened and watched. They were all good people...yet they got stuck because they understandably had poor grasp of group dynamics. At an opportune moment, I stepped in and made a group-as-a-whole statement. I won't quote it verbatim since it won't mean much out of context, yet, paraphrasing, it was along these lines: "It seems to me that the committee is in agreement about its basic goals yet has gotten stuck by straying a bit on to topics which aren't central to the goals and which are pet theories. I suggest we just stay with the facts which fit with our goals." Of course I was subtly or politely saying: "Hey, c'mon, cut it out, let go of your pet irrelevancies and let's stick to the job". In any case, there was a palpable shift, and an obvious nonverbal agreement [nodding, etc] and we got back on track and made good progress in the time remaining.

This is one example of how we can bring our group therapy skills to community endeavors, be it by process statements like the above or by owning feelings in one's self or recognizing them in others or by mediating between conflicting parties, etc. Gaie Houston addresses this challenge and the analogy she uses is "I have a sense of being something like a visiting aunt" [1996,p. 279]; I interpret that she means she is part of the group, yet somewhat more objective and mature, focusing on the good of the many [the whole] rather than on herself. I trust the reader can visualize herself in similar situations and using her group therapy skills to advantage.

Educational Applications

Most formal education takes place in classrooms [of course nowadays there is a good deal online, too]...and every aggregate of students in a classroom, along with the teacher, is a group. Not a therapy group, of course, though a case could be made for considering it at least a growth group. In any case an educational or learning group. Therefore the principles of group dynamics apply and the principles of gestalt therapy are very relevant. This was recognized

149

long ago by George Brown at the University of California at Santa Barbara, although he used the term 'confluent education' most often, yet clearly his writings refer to gestalt therapy [1975]. His focus was more on attention to the affective life of students, particularly elementary grade students, and less to the group dynamic aspects of the situation. Following Brown, both Rona Laves [1980] and John Flynn [1980] addressed similar issues with regard to the college classroom. Flynn pointed out that Gestalt group therapists promote awareness and autonomy and that an educator can do the same utilizing an experimental and experiential approach. The details are beyond the scope of this treatise, yet those interested in this problem can well benefit from Flynn's thoughtful erudite discussion. Laves focuses on the passivity bred in students by our educational system and indicates how emphasizing gestalt principles of awareness, contact, the balance of safety [or support] and risk, excitement and experimentation can lead to a more active role on the part of the student – and beyond that growth in that area of being. Again I refer you to her chapter.

Epilogue - Lincoln and his Cabinet

"O Captain! My Captain,
our fearful trip is done.
The ship has weather'd every rack.
The prize we sought is won.
But I with mournful tread,
walk the deck my captain lies,
fallen, cold and dead."

Walt Whitman

At about the same time that I started working on this opus, somebody gave me the book *Team of Rivals* [2005] by the eminent historian Doris Kearns Goodwin. The book is a magnificent study of how Lincoln selected, maintained, nourished, managed and related to his cabinet. In addition to the fact that I have been a Lincoln buff ever since the first time I read Carl Sandburg's six-volume life of Lincoln when I was twelve, I found the book fascinating from a group leader's standpoint.

As the title of Goodwin's book indicates, there was a lot of rivalry among this group. When Lincoln put himself forward in the Republican primary of 1860, he was initially considered to be running behind three other much better known candidates: the New York senator William H. Seward, the Ohio governor Salmon P. Chase, and Missouri's distinguished elder statesman Edward Bates. Obviously Lincoln – against great odds – won the nomination. Many were disappointed. Ralph Waldo Emerson, for instance, recalled "we heard the result coldly and sadly. It seemed too rash, on a purely local reputation, to build so grave a trust in such anxious times". The three men he defeated all considered him incompetent and certainly inferior to themselves.

And then of course Lincoln won the ensuing election and as president-elect his first task was to select a cabinet. Remarkably and unprecedently, the first three he tapped for the most important positions were the three who had just been his disdainful rivals: for Secretary of State, Seward; for Secretary of the Treasury, Chase; and for Attorney General, Bates. He then offered five of the six remaining posts to members or former members of the rival political party, the Democrats, against Seward's remonstrations. So there it was: a team of rivals, with rivalries criss-crossing in all directions.

Over time he led this group into a well-functioning nation-saving team. How did he do this? You could read Goodwin's 900-page book, which would be a wise and most satisfying course. In case you don't though, I'll give you the short version with a look at the group dynamic and gestalt approaches involved.

According to Goodwin, and according to everything we know about Lincoln, he achieved this through kindness, sensitivity, compassion, honesty and empathy, not to mention shrewdness and strength of will and purpose. Lincoln himself had experienced a great deal of trauma and pain in his life, at one time being close to suicide. He trudged and fought through these bad times, and I think it safe to say that as a result he had a great deal of compassion and self-awareness – self-achieved of course without the benefit of therapy. So he had many of the qualifications of an outstanding leader.

In his meetings with his cabinet, he was careful to see that each man had his say on the issues at hand, and he always gave full and careful attention to dissenting viewpoints *[involving the whole group, respectfulness]*. He shared his doubts and worries [*self-revelation*] and when in doubt often went with the majority [*democratic style*]. On the other hand when he completely and clearly disagreed with the majority he made an unpopular decision [*judicious responsibility*]. He frequently soothed and nurtured hurt feelings in acceptable and clever ways *[giving as much support as necessary]* and often charged cabinet members with strong responsibility and authority [*and as little as possible*].

One vignette may give a sense of this great man's consummate group leadership style. Early in the war, the South [aka the Confederacy] was hopeful of getting the support of England, which depended on Confederate cotton to supply their cotton mills in Manchester and elsewhere. Accordingly, the Confederacy assigned two prominent southerners to travel to England to argue its case for formal recognition by England, which would have multiple ramifications. The North [or Union] got wind of this and intercepted the British ship carrying the Southerners, boarded it and took the two captive. The British were furious at this "outrage on the British flag…. demanding reparation and apology and the return of the prisoners"

[Goodwin, p. 197]. Failure to do so might lead to the British declaring war on the Union, which would undoubtedly be more than Union could handle – the Union was already having great difficulty with the Confederacy.

The cabinet met on Christmas morning to discuss the situation. Only Seward saw the wisdom of giving in to England and returning the prisoners. All but one of the others – including Lincoln --wanted to refuse. Some made statements like "Rather than consent to the liberation of these men, I would sacrifice everything I possess" and "Returning the prisoners would be gall and wormwood" [Ibid, p. 199]. After four hours still only one member agreed with Seward. Lincoln sent them home, stipulating that overnight Seward would prepare a written draft with all his reasons why the prisoners should be returned. He, Lincoln himself, would prepare an argument for the other side.

The next day Seward brought his 26-page draft as instructed and read it to the assembled cabinet. "The dispatch was unanimously adopted. After the meeting Seward asked

Lincoln why he had not presented the argument for the other side.

With a smile, Lincoln replied 'I found I could not make an argument that would satisfy my own mind, and that proved to me your ground was the right one' " [Ibid, p. 200]. His ego in check, he allowed the group the call...and the Union was saved.

I rest my case.

Appendix A. Handouts for Clients

(Feel free to borrow, steal, modify these handouts)

Handout # 1:   THE HERE-AND-NOW
[OR INTERACTIVE] GROUP

Overview: These groups are an exciting, difficult and powerful vehicle for personal growth. On them you learn from your interactions with other group members about your interpersonal style, including your ways of interrupting and distorting contact. And these groups provide an immediate opportunity to experiment and to risk new ways of being with others. Often the groups provide a sense of closeness and belonging, an opportunity to connect and to grow. And the assumption is that you will learn to transfer from the group to the rest of your life (more on this later [see consultations]).

On the down side, these groups are not recommended as the therapy of choice to work directly on specific problems being experienced in primary relationships, work or health. The group focuses almost exclusively on what is happening now in this situation. To work on those problems it is recommended to utilize individual, couples or family therapy.

The Group Process: In the here-and-now group you can expect:

*the leader will draw the group's attention to feelings within the group and toward other members, individually and in subgroups

*awareness of opportunities for and fear of innovative behavior

*opportunities for and expectation of each member participating emotionally, cognitively and behaviorally, although each member is free to work at her/his own pace

*various techniques and methods, such as rounds, experiments and risks, which will become clearer as we work – again at your own pace

Recommendations: In order to get the most out of the group experience, it is recommended that members:

*focus on what is happening now, in this group
*become aware of their counterproductive fixed and stuck patterns
*seek and take opportunities to try out innovative behavior
*come five minutes early to get centered
*miss no sessions unless unavoidable
*fill out group logs after sessions

Consultations: For those members not in individual therapy with the leader, it is desirable to have an occasional individual consultation. This will help provide direction for transferring growth to the rest of your life, which after all is the ultimate person of the endeavor. Also this will provide an opportunity to discuss anything you absolutely cannot bring up [yet] in the group and to develop strategies for the group.

Relationships outside of group. Contact between members outside of group is neither encouraged nor discouraged, yet if anything of significance occurs it is agreed that it is grist for the mill and may legitimately be brought up in group. Failure to do so would be a violation of the group's code.

Extended Sessions: Occasionally the group may occasionally schedule an extended session [all-day or weekend] if all are in agreement.

Physical Violence: Although the group is not a social event and raw expression of feeling is the norm, no physical violence will be tolerated. This does not preclude discussion of such desires.

Handout # 2. Group Therapy Agreement

To achieve maximum gains from your group therapy, I recommend your acknowledgment and agreement to the following:

Sessions will take place most _____s from _____to _____. We will each make every effort to be begin sessions on time. In the event of an unavoidable absence we will notify the others as soon as possible. If notice cannot be given before the sessions, then as soon as possible after it. Four absences during the calendar year beginning Jan 1st will be exempt from a charge. These may be for any reasons although absences are subject to therapeutic exploration when relevant. Additional absences for any reason may be charged for

Membership: this is a group of _____ members and ___ therapist[s]. It is open-ended, that is of no fixed duration, and open to new members as old members leave.

Therapeutic orientation: this is a therapy group, not a social group, therefore we will not observe all the customs of social decorum. Members may express feelings and thoughts openly, sometimes interrupting one another. Should the group be of the kind called "interactive", the ground rules that apply will be observed, after being explained.

Contact between or among members outside of group is neither encouraged nor discouraged; however it is agreed that if contact occurs, anything of significance or problematic or disturbing will be brought into the group for the benefit of all and is, in other words, grist for the therapeutic mill; thus privacy or secrecy may not be legitimately be demand or requested by the members involved.

Confidentiality: we will not discuss the group with outsiders in any way that will jeopardize anyone's confidentiality or privacy, except:
*in instances of imminent danger to anyone
*if the therapist is required by law or HIPPA regulations to disclose

Individual therapy sessions between members and any therapist are governed by the rules of confidentiality.

Physical activity: this is primarily a verbal group with some physical activities and experiments according to each member's choice. Noone will be pressured to participate in these; they will be offered and the choice is the member's, although the opportunity to explore reluctances may also be offered. In no case will anyone attack anyone else physically. Any violation of this rule will certainly be subject to therapeutic exploration and in any extreme instance may be a cause for discontinuance in the group [a euphemism for being kicked out. Behavior has consequences. However this is extremely rare.

Fee: The fee for this service is $_____/session. Payment will be made regularly and responsibly and departures from this may be brought up in the group for therapeutic exploration by either party. The therapist will present a bill shortly after the first of each month for the previous month and payment is expected by the end of the month; thus payment for January is expected by the end of February, etc.

Termination: We agree that staying in the group until significant gains have been achieved is desirable; at times this may be difficult to do. Yet it is understood that on average two to three years of participation is recommended, although this is just a rule of thumb. In any case, leaving the group abruptly is generally counterproductive for all, so that, if at all possible it is desirable to allow sufficient time to process and understand this step as well as giving everyone an opportunity for relative closure and to say goodbye. A month's notice is therefore agreed upon.

All of the above is subject to review and renegotiation, preferably in the group.

_____
Bud Feder, Therapist   Date

_____
Client   Date

Handout # 3:   The "Co-therapist" Role: A Guide for Clients.

Purpose: During group therapy sessions, clients often assist me [the therapist], thus they assume informally, for the moment, a co-therapist [or perhaps more accurately an assistant-therapist] role. This guide will assist client-"therapists" to function more productively.

I.   Questions Clients often try to help each other with questions, such as "Why did you let your Jill just push you around" or "Why don't you want to do that experiment?", etc. If the client already knows these answers, telling them to you won't help. Instead ask questions which promote awareness, such as "What are you feeling when you hear Jill? " or "What can you do different in response to Jill?" or "What do you get out of avoiding that experiment?". If you take note of the kind of questions I ask, that will help you.

II.   Support: it is natural to want to support or comfort a fellow member whom you care about, particularly when she is in great pain. If she is done working, that's fine; if she is in the middle of a necessary heavy piece of work. Then wait. Don't deprive her of a needed, though difficult, experience [experience means to "travel through, then out of" -- and that's therapy; excessive group support is just expensive temporary comfort. Keep this in mind if at times I ask you to hold off.

III.   Advice: Avoid telling another what you think he ought to do. Most of the time, you will be wasting your breath. He's probably heard the like often enough outside of group and it hasn't led to anything. It is better for the client to come to his own conclusions. Also this will avoid   time-consuming   debates   and intellectualizing.

IV.   Interpretations: Sometimes once client "sees" another's p[picture [or thinks she does] before the other client sees it herself. If so, hold on to it; you'll find out if you're right when she gets to it. Don't rush in with "Oh, I see -- you're afraid of men" or worse "You're afraid of men because....".

V.   Feedback: There are two kinds of feedback which are very helpful. The first of these is when you tell the other what you experience when he does a certain thing or acts in a certain way. Examples are: "When you scream at me like that, I want nothing to do with you...or I feel scared...or I want to beat your face in", etc. Give him feedback on how he affects you.

The second helpful kind of feedback is when you simply reflect back to him what you observe, such as: Right now I see you beating on your leg with your fist" or "I notice how soft your voice becomes when you say you are angry". No advice or suggestions or interpretations – just observations.

Handout # 4. Embrace/Avoid

Embrace

*NOTICING YOUR BODILY SENSATIONS
*NOTICING YOUR THOUGHTS, IMAGES, MEMORIES
*EXPRESSING ALOUD ALL OF THE ABOVE
*NOTICING YOUR IMPULSES
*EXPRESSING THEM [VERBALLY]
*CREATING EXPERIMENTS FOR YOURSELF AND OTHERS
*PROVIDING HONEST FEEDBACK EVEN IF UNPLEASANT
*MAKING STATEMENTS

AVOID:

*STORY-TELLING
*REMINISCING
*GENERALIZING ["I USUALLY...OFTEN...SOMETIMES"]
*COMPARING THE IMMEDIATE EXPERIENCE WITH SIMILAR ONES
*GIVING ADVICE
*DEFLECTING THROUGH HUMOR
*ASKING QUESTIONS WHICH DISGUISE STATEMENTS
*ASKING "WHY'
*MISSING SESSIONS AND COMING LATE
*GIVING PREMATURE COMFORT [IN THE MIDDLE OF WORK]

Group Therapy Log

I. What did you work on this session?   How far did you get?   What is next?   How can apply or play with this issue in your everyday life?

II. Give any other impressions or feelings about today's session: other members, format, methods applied, experiments, etc

III. Is there anything of significance going on in your life which you want me to know?

IV. Add any other comments, suggestions, information, etc

Appendix B.
A Selected Annotated Reading List

Here are a few items I think are particularly useful...there are of course many more:

Group vs. Individual Therapy by Fritz Perls, originally appeared in an obscure journal called *Etc: A review of general Semantics,* Vol. 34, #3, 1967, pp. 306-312. In the article Fritz argues – unconvincingly from my view – that all individual therapy will soon be obsolete and replaced by group therapy, as more economical and more efficient. His discussion, if not persuasive, is very interesting both from a clinical and a historic point of view. If you can't find it, contact me and I will send you a copy [eventually].

Opening Doors by Dan Rosenblatt [1975] NY: Harper & Row. An easy to read little book, the second half of which is devoted to group therapy. It is a cogent and useful and has a distinct NY flavor, i.e. it is somewhat rambly and unsystematic.

Creative Process in Gestalt Therapy by Joe Zinker [1977] NY: Brunner/Mazel. This is a delightful book and Ch 7 is particularly relevant. Colorfully written and very rich with regard to insights and methods.

Beyond the Hot Seat: Gestalt Approaches to Group. [1980;]. Bud Feder & Ruth Ronall, Eds. NY: Brunner/Mazel [original hardcover edition]; and New Orleans: Gestalt Institute Press [handy plastic binding version]. As mentioned earlier, it is still the only Gestalt Therapy book devoted exclusively to Gestalt groups, and though it has some weaknesses it has been very influential in the Gestalt community and has some outstanding contributions in the theoretical chapters. It is also valuable in providing clear presentations of various applications: marathons, training, education, etc.

Beyond the Hot Seat Revisited: Gestalt Approaches to Group, (2006) Bud Feder & Jon Frew, editors. Gestalt Institute Press. Metairie, LA.

The Practice of Gestalt Therapy in Groups by Jon Frew , [1988] in the *Gestalt Journal,* 11(1), pp. 77-96. This article builds on a survey done by me in 1974 [unpublished] and provides factual information about such aspects as group sizes, change factors, therapeutic approaches, etc. A follow-up survey has been done by the two of us and will be published in the Fall, 2006 issue of the *Gestalt Review.* In general, Jon Frew has

178

written many fine articles on gestalt groups and in my opinion writes more comprehensively, cogently and satisfactorily on this topic than anyone else.

"An Overview of the Theory and Practice of Gestalt Group Process"[1992] by Mary Ann Huckaby, a chapter in *Gestalt Therapy*, E. Nevis, Ed. NY: Gardner Press. This contains much more about theory than practice and is a good cognitive introduction, in contrast to Rosenblatt's more experiential style.

"The Healing Through Relationship in an Interactive Gestalt Group" [1996] by Jay Earley, a chapter *in A Living Legacy of Fritz and Laura Perls:* Contemprary Case Studies. B. Feder & R. Ronall, Eds. New Orleans: Gestalt Institute Press

"An Extended Group Experience" [1996] by Jack Aylward, another chapter in *Legacy.* This chapter first gives historical background to the uses of extended groups [or marathons] and describes in a very lively way such a group led by Jack and me.

"Gestalt Group Therapy" [2005]by Paul Schoenberg with Bud Feder. A chapter in an outstanding new textbook, *Gestalt Therapy: Theory, History and Practice.* Woldt, A. & Toman, S. Thousand Oaks, CA: Sage Publications

References

Angyal, A. [1982] *Neurosis and Treatment: A Holistic Theory.* N.Y.: Da Capo Press

Aylward, J. [1996] An Extended Group Experience. In B. Feder & R. Ronall [Eds.] *A Living Legacy of Fritz and Laura Perls: Contemporary Case Studies.* New Orleans: Gestalt Institute Press

Bedi, R. P. [2005] Critical Incidents in the Formation of the Therapeutic Alliance from the Client's Perspective. *Psychotherapy: Therapy, Research, Practice,* Vol. 42, No. 3, pp. 311-23

Brown, G. I., Yeomans, T., & Grizzard, L. [Eds.] [1975] *The Live Classroom: Innovations through Confluent Education and Gestalt.* N.Y.: Viking Press

Cartwright, D. and Zander, A. [1956]. *Group Dynamics: Research and Theory* Evanston, IL: Row, Peterson and Co.

Elson, M. [1986] *Self Psychology in Clinical Social Work.* N.Y.: W. W. Norton & Co.

Feder, B. [2004] Dual Relationships: A Gestalt Therapy Perspective. *Gestalt Review,* Vol. 8, No. 2, 135-45.

Feder, B. [1980] Responsibility in Gestalt Therapy. *The Gestalt Journal,* Vol. 1, pp. 46-50

Feder, B. [1980] Safety and Danger in the Gestalt Group. In B. Feder & R. Ronall [Eds.] *Beyond the Hot Seat: Gestalt Approaches to Group.* New Orleans: Gestalt Institute Press

Feder, B. & Ronall, R (Eds.) [1980] *Beyond the Hot Seat: Gestalt Approaches to Group.* New Orleans: Gestalt Institute Press

Flynn, J. D. [1980] Educating for Autonomy. In B. Feder & R. Ronall [Eds.] *Beyond the Hot Seat: Gestalt Approaches to Group.* New Orleans: Gestalt Institute Press

Goodwin, D. K. [2005] *Team of Rivals.* NY: Simon & Schuster

Greenberg, E. and Hahn, A. [2001] Group Therapy and Disorders of the Self in *The Masterson Newsletter*. NY: The Masterson Institute

Houston, G. [1996] Politics and Personalities in Gestalt and Other Fields. In *A Living Legacy of Fritz and Laura Perls: Contemporary Case Studies*. B. Feder & R. Ronall [Eds]. New Orleans: Gestalt Institute Press

Ike,B.W. [1987] Man's limited sympathy as a consequence of his evolution in small kin groups. In V. Reynolds, B.W. Ike, I. Wine, and M. Flohr [Eds.], *The Sociobiology of Ethnocentrism*. Athens, GA: University of Georgia Press

Kepner, E. [1980] Gestalt Group Process. In Feder, B. & Ronall, R. (Eds.). *Beyond the Hot Seat: Gestalt Approaches to Group*. New Orleans: Gestalt Institute Press

Klepner, P. [1996] Living, Loving and Laughter. In B. Feder & R. Ronall [Eds.] *A Living Legacy of Fritz and Laura Perls: Contemporary Case Studies*. New Orleans: Gestalt Institute Press

Laves, R. G. [1980] Contact and Boundary: Creating a Nontraditional Classroom. In B. Feder & R. Ronall [Eds.] *Beyond the Hot Seat: Gestalt Approaches to Group.* New Orleans: Gestalt Institute Press

Lewin, K., Lippitt, R., & White, R. K. [1939] Patterns of aggressive behavior in experimentally created 'social climates'. *Journal of Social Psychology,* 10, 271- 299.

Lilliengren, P. A Model of Therapeutic Action Grounded in the Patient's View of Curative and Hindering Factors in Psychotherapy. *Psychotherapy: Theory, Research, Practice,* Vol. 42, No. 3, pp. 324-39.

Melnick, J., Nevis, S. M., and Melnick, G. [1994] Therapeutic Ethics: A Gestalt Perspective. *The British Gestalt Journal,* Vol 3, pp. 105-13.

Mintz, E. [1980] The Gestalt Therapy Marathon. In B. Feder & R. Ronall [Eds.] *Beyond the Hot Seat: Gestalt Approaches to Group.* New Orleans: Gestalt Institute Press

Perls, F.S. [1973] *The Gestalt Approach and Eyewitness to Therapy.* N. Y.: Bantam Books

Perls, F. S., Hefferline, R., & Goodman, P. [1994] *Gestalt Therapy: Excitement and Growth in the Human Personality* (Rev. Ed.). N Y: Julian Press

Perls, L. [1992] Conceptions and Misconceptions of Gestalt Therapy. In *Living at the Boundary.* Highland, NY: Gestalt Journal Press

Schoenberg, P. [1999] *The Impact of gestalt group Therapy on persons with Borderline Personality.* Ph. D. Dissertation. Kent,Ohio:Kent State University

Schoenberg, P. & Feder, B. [2005] Gestalt Therapy in Groups. In A. Woldt & S. Toman *Gestalt Therapy: History, Theory and Practice.* Thousand Oaks, CA: Sage Publications

Slavson, S. R. [1970] *An Introduction to Group Therapy.* N.Y.: International Universities Press

Sullivan, H. S. [1945] *Conceptions of Modern Psychiatry.* N.Y.: Wm. Alanson White Psychiatric Foundation

Wheelis, A. [1975]   *How People Change.* N.Y.:
Harper Colophon Books

www.ingramcontent.com/pod-product-compliance
Lightning Source LLC
Chambersburg PA
CBHW070648290526
45790CB00001B/227